NELSON

NELSON

by

Richard Hough

Park Lane Press

FRONTISPIECE Nelson painted by Leonardo
Guzzardi, 1799.
ENDPAPERS Eighteenth-century English coverlet
embroidered in silks and gold.

∽ Contents ∽

1

The Making of
the Sailor

The barge was awash with blood, and the dead and mortally wounded lay in grotesque attitudes in the scuppers and sprawled over the gunwales. The Spanish gunboat alongside – four times the size of the British barge – was in an even worse state. The Spaniards – the 'Dons' – had outnumbered the British thirty to thirteen. Now most of them lay dead, shot by the one fusillade the British sailors had fired at point-blank range, pierced by sword and slashed by sabre.

Still the Spanish commander, Don Miguel Tyrason, fought bravely on against this wild foe, who should have fled or surrendered at the first contact. Instead, these British had appeared to welcome their disadvantage as if it were a spur to certain victory. They were led by an officer, small of stature, white-haired and past his first youth, but the most eager to leap forward, sword in hand, when the two boats were laid alongside one another.

It could be said that this British officer, Horatio Nelson, bore a charmed life. But there were several present who, through the smoke and tumult of hand-to-hand fighting, observed a stalwart sailor, the barge's coxswain John Sykes, as close alongside him as were the two Spanish and British boats, parrying enemy thrusts and blows without regard for his own safety. A sword stab that would have gone clean through Nelson was parried one moment, the next this gallant sailor used his bare arm to protect him from a cutlass sweep that could have taken off his head, and then himself fell to join the dead and wounded in the bottom of the boat.

It seemed that no power on earth could have held back this British company. Into the Spanish gunboat they swarmed, over the bodies, pressing the Spaniards back towards their own commander, who continued to urge them on until the spirit went out of the survivors.

Then, in the centre of this bloody scene and amid the screams and

Nelson's encounter with the Spanish gunboat at Cadiz in 1797, painted by Richard Westall.

7

cries of the wounded, Don Miguel surrendered and handed over his sword to the small, bespattered, panting English admiral.

Earlier, Don Miguel had been astonished to recognize an admiral's barge inside the harbour, the admiral himself directing the fire of his ships' guns against the port and city of Cadiz, and had briefly blessed his good fortune when the barge with its handful of sailors appeared to welcome a fight. At first, the Spanish weight of numbers nearly resulted in what had appeared inevitable, and Don Miguel had almost taken the barge.

Instead, on this morning of 3 July 1797, it was the little British barge that towed the Spanish gunboat back towards the flagship *Theseus*, with its cargo of dead and wounded Spaniards. There were British dead and wounded, too, and the admiral was holding his coxswain in his arms. 'Sykes, I cannot forget this,' said Nelson, who knew that he would now be lying with the other corpses but for the gallantry of this Lincolnshire man.

'Thank God, Sir, you are safe,' muttered the wounded sailor.

Amid the smoke of the bombardment, the forts, the crenellated towers, the church spires and handsome white mansions of Cadiz fell astern of the barge. Nelson was feeling the sense of triumph and elation he always experienced after a dangerous action – 'A glorious death is to be envied,' he once told his alarmed wife. And a week later wrote to her of this naval battle in miniature, 'My late Affair here will not, I believe, lower me in the opinion of the world. I have had flattery enough to make me vain, and success enough to make me confident.'

And, in much later years, he wrote of this period that 'perhaps my personal courage was more conspicuous than at any other part of my life'.

The courage was never to diminish, let alone to run out. But what of the luck that, like John Sykes, seemed always to hold so closely to his side in battle? Shortly after this desperate fight off Cadiz, it seemed as if it might be running out on him after all . . .

Let us go back some thirty years. A frail-looking boy sits on the bank of a north Norfolk river, legs in well-worn breeches stretched out before him, eyes fixed on the coasters warping their way up or slipping down with the tide, quick to distinguish single-masted wherry with gaff mainsail from two-masted lugger, fore-and-aft rigged hoy from two-masted buss trailing herring stench as it labours its way to the wharf with its barrels of North Sea fish.

The port is Burnham Overy Staithe, noisy at midday with the sounds of voices and occasional cracks of laughter and obscenity, as boats are made fast and untied, sails hoisted and lowered, winch cables secured, a load of bricks for King's Lynn raised from a dray, a dozen sacks of good wheat from the Holkham estates hoisted aboard a sloop to join a dozen casks of clay in the hold.

A miniature of Nelson aged eight.

On the quayside, in the lanes set back from it and the main street beyond, there are sailors and labourers, some full of beer and others in search of it, farmers and men of commerce deep in trade, women gossiping, children, both younger and older than this watching boy, fighting and playing.

But it is the shipping that holds the boy's attention. If he stands up, he can see down the creek almost to the estuary among the sand dunes and salt marshes. If he climbs a little way up the hill south of the town, he will see more shipping far out to sea: brigantines tacking and wearing, perhaps a Dutch bilander (he will recognize it at once by its lateen-rigged mainmast) bowling before the brisk north-westerly, heading for The Hague and home.

Here, where most men live on the land, growing and tending and

breeding or taking from it gravel and clay or baking bricks in the kilns – here one is as near to a boat as the next cornfield. Here a boy will grow up to work on the land or on the sea. There is no other occupation.

This small boy – Horatio Nelson, son of the rector at Burnham Thorpe – is destined to retain his attachment to this part of north-west Norfolk and his romantic love of the land for all his restless life. But it is the sea that has seized his imagination, as tightly as the cables securing that sloop to the wharf ring. The sea which he can smell from the Parsonage, the sea with its ever-changing mood and colour, the sea with its marvellous range of ships and boats from massive 100-gun three-decked naval men-of-war to little fishing boats that nip in and out of this harbour like hungry bees after nectar for an hour or two at a time. It is the sea that has claimed

The Parsonage House, Burnham Thorpe, painted by Francis Pocock; Nelson may be the young boy in the foreground waving a flag.

10

this undersized, pale, fair-haired little boy; claimed him hook, line and sinker, as these fishermen of Overy Staithe might remark in their rich Norfolk accent.

From time to time inherited genes – like the roll of the dice, roulette ball, the fall of cards – play a hundred-million-to-one trick, and turn up a Michelangelo, a William Shakespeare, a Napoleon Bonaparte, a George Washington, who survives the commonplace diseases of infancy and by a further coincidence of time and circumstance and the support of friends can exercise his special genius to ultimate capacity.

There appeared to be nothing in the stars on Friday 29 September 1758, at the parsonage of Burnham Thorpe in Norfolk, to indicate that a child of exceptional quality, destined for mammoth achievement, was born to the rector's wife, Catherine. On the contrary, the omens were not propitious. Catherine Nelson had already given birth to five children, none of whom had shown any unusual quality, and the first two boys had both died in infancy. (The second of these had also been baptized Horatio, so the future hero was not even the first in the family to bear this name.)

Six weeks later this second Horatio Nelson was carried to the church of All Saints and there baptized. Beside the font was a lectern that would one day be replaced by another made from one of the timbers of his most famous flagship, HMS *Victory*.

The baptism was conducted in the presence of the infant's spon-

All Saints Church, Burnham Thorpe, painted by M. E. Cotman in 1840; Nelson was baptized there by his father, rector of the parish.

FAR LEFT The Reverend
Edmund Nelson.
LEFT Nelson's mother,
Catherine Suckling,
aged eighteen, painted
before her marriage.
FACING PAGE The
Paston School, North
Walsham, where Nelson
went, aged eleven.

sor, the second Baron Walpole of Wolterton, the son of the great
statesman and First Minister Sir Robert Walpole, who had been a
brother to Catherine's grandmother. It was the only hint, and a
distant one, that there were any special qualities in the maternal
line. The paternal line could best be described as respectable, the
rector's grandmother having been born the daughter of a Cambridge
baker.

From his mother, Horatio Nelson inherited, among other qualities, tenderness and sentimentality, but she died while he was still
a child.

There is strength and character in the portrait of Catherine
Nelson. But the will and inspiration, the self-confidence, dedicated
patriotism and sense of purpose, came from his father. His father
gave him other qualities, some deriving from his own unquestion-
ing faith, like his compassion for the poor and underprivileged.
Edmund Nelson had graduated from Cambridge University, and
his scholarship, in the form of a worldly knowledge and a lucid
prose style, brushed off on his son. So did his waggish humour.
Edmund Nelson farmed thirty acres or so of glebe land with uneven
success, and this activity of Horatio's early childhood planted the
romantic love of the soil which rested uneasily all his life beside his
passionate love of the sea and could be manifested only in his last
years of fame.

The two extremes of wealth and poverty, of the great estates at Raynham, Houghton and Holkham, of innumerable hovels where even bread was often hard to come by, lay all about the Burnham Thorpe parsonage. At a time when 'redistribution of wealth' had never been heard of, the Nelsons of Burnham Thorpe might be on social terms with the wealthy gentry, and even related to them, yet still suffer from poverty. The Rector's living was modest, his children ever increasing in numbers, eleven in all, the mother dying in 1767, nine months after the birth of her last child. There was much talk of class aspirations, and of money, at the Parsonage. It was no wonder Horatio grew up with a longing for social acceptance, and for wealth. Although he was to become comparatively rich, his class sensitivity was to remain with him through all his years of fame.

There was talk, too, of mitigating the family's financial straits by apprenticing out the girls, a resort of the penurious middle classes. Horatio, following the custom of his class and background, was sent away to boarding schools in Norfolk, starting at the Royal Grammar School at Norwich, receiving a good grounding in the 'three Rs', in the classics and French. A number of stories, some true, others no doubt apocryphal, were told of his boyhood in Norfolk after his death. Several of them concerned his hobby of bird's-nesting. Once, found when lost on a search beside an impassable stream by his grandmother, he is supposed to have answered her anxious enquiry that he must have been alarmed, 'I never saw fear. What is it?' The claim, if not the story, is certainly true.

As daughters might be apprenticed to milliners, it was commonplace for sons as young as twelve to be sent to sea with the Royal Navy. Unusual in Nelson's case was his own initiative. At some time around Christmas 1770, he happened to read in the local newspaper that his late mother's brother, Captain Maurice Suckling R.N., was about to commission the ship of the line HMS *Raisonnable* after a long period on half pay.

LEFT Nelson's uncle, Captain Maurice Suckling, was instrumental in helping him join the Royal Navy. BELOW A drawing by Thomas Rowlandson showing sailors on board the man-of-war, *Hector*, relaxing in port.

The rector was away at Bath at the time, but Horatio's elder brother, William, wrote on his behalf to tell him that he 'would like to go with my uncle Maurice to sea'. The Reverend Edmund Nelson passed on his son's request with some relief. Captain Suckling's response was typically robust and saltily hearty:

> What has poor Horace done, who is so weak, that he above all the rest should be sent to rough it out to sea? But let him come; and the first time we go into action, a cannon-ball may knock off his head, and provide for him at once.

By themselves, inherited qualities are rarely enough to bring out the hundred-million-to-one trick. However, for all his life, Nelson was blessed with friends. His first was Uncle Maurice. Catherine's brother was rich and well endowed with courage and intelligence, too. His portrait shows the same full lips, the wide-set intelligent eyes, the same full nose as his sister. To Nelson he had always been an heroic figure, and 21 October was celebrated in the family as the anniversary of Uncle Maurice's greatest victory, a year before Horatio was born. Now, indirectly, Maurice was to be instrumental in bringing about another occasion for celebration on the same day half a century later, when the boy he had once sponsored died at Trafalgar.

In an age of patronage, when it was considered a duty to help those for whom you had agreed to be responsible, Maurice Suckling almost exceeded his duties. From the first meeting between the small, pale twelve-year-old midshipman on board the *Raisonnable* at Chatham, Captain Suckling recognized unusual qualities in this nephew. Nelson had to rough it with the other midshipmen. The contrast with the life and freedom of the Parsonage could not have been stranger. Except for the officers, conditions at sea in the eighteenth century were appalling by any standards: the confinement; the never-ending and often violent movement of the ship; the stench of unwashed bodies, tar, hemp, tallow, smoke from the stoves; food of appalling inedibility; a daily routine, especially in northern waters, of struggle against the elements, of shinning up to the dizzy heights of the yards to make or take in sail; of never being dry for days on end; of conforming to the harsh discipline and ferocious physical demands at the risk of reprimand, demotion and, all too frequently, a flogging at the grating.

For five months on this his first voyage, the young Nelson endured the high seas, and was very seasick; endured the cruel bully-
ing, the foul food and arduous daily routine without complaint.
And at the end of it all proclaimed that he wanted no other life.

The *Raisonnable* had been commissioned because of the risk of
war with Spain. When the threat disappeared, the big ship was paid
off, and Suckling was instead given command of a guardship in the
Thames Estuary. This would not provide any sort of life for a young
lad, the Captain decided. Young Horatio must get more and wider
experience, learn navigation and small-boat work, mathematics,
the use of hydrographical charts and signalling. In peace, this
could best be obtained at sea in a merchantman, and the sight of
new shores would broaden the boy's mind as well as improve his
geography. This education, mainly in the West Indies, helped make
him into 'a practical seaman', as he described himself a year later.

The making of the sailor now went ahead fast. On Nelson's return
from his first long voyage in foreign waters, he rejoined Suckling's
guardship at Chatham. On board, he continued his training in navigation theory, and in the ship's cutter and decked longboat learned
the practice of navigation in one of the best training grounds in the

ABOVE A marine
compass of 1775.

16

world, the tricky Thames and its estuary. 'Thus by degrees I became a good pilot,' he wrote later of this period, 'from Chatham to the Tower of London, down the Swin and the North Foreland; and confident of myself amongst rocks and sands, which has many times been a great comfort to me.'

The 1770s was the most important and exciting decade of exploration in history. The French, the Dutch and the Spaniards all undertook great voyages at this period. But no people voyaged so far, nor opened up so much of the world, as the British. George Anson's earlier circumnavigation in 1743, which made him rich and famous, was only a forerunner. Samuel Wallis and Philip Carteret did much to chart the Pacific Ocean. James Cook in three remarkable voyages discovered innumerable groups of islands, and charted for the first time the east coast of Australia and the two islands of New Zealand. On his last and fatal voyage he was ordered to search for an eastern

ABOVE Thomas Rowlandson frequently made sketches of the Thames at Greenwich; this view, drawn in 1795, shows the arrival of a ferryboat at low tide at Greenwich stairs, next to the Salutation Tavern: the Royal Hospital for Seamen, now the Royal Naval College, is in the background.

entrance to the fabled North West Passage, which had already cost so many lives.

A short route to the riches of the East had been a dream that had led to the first circumnavigation by Magellan's expedition in 1520-2. Now there were rumours of an Arctic expedition to search for a North East Passage, north of Russia. It was called a scientific enterprise, but the glory and benefit resulting from the charting of a northern route to the Pacific would be enormous.

Details of the expedition reached Nelson and the other eager midshipmen of the guardship. Its commander was to be Captain Constantine Phipps, there were to be two vessels, tough old bomb ketches, the *Racehorse* and *Carcass*, and they were to explore closer to the North Pole than ever before. Then the fatal blow: no boys were to be taken, the risks being too great.

This only spurred Nelson on to make greater efforts and to use all the influence he could bring to bear. At length, he discovered a way round the prohibition: both ships' commanders could take a personal servant, and Nelson was made coxswain of the captain's gig of the *Racehorse*.

The expedition departed in the early summer of 1773, and forced its way to within 10 degrees of the Pole before being halted by the ice, which at one point threatened to lock in the two ships for the winter.

There is a well-known anecdote about Nelson – not yet fifteen –

RIGHT The *Racehorse* and *Carcass* trapped in the polar ice during the Arctic expedition in which Nelson took part; sailors can be seen hauling a boat over the ice to reach open water.

Nelson's famous attack on a polar bear during the expedition.

among the frozen Polar wastes. The *Racehorse*'s captain recounted later that he had been informed that Nelson, with a companion, had stolen out onto the ice on a polar-bear hunt. The boys were soon missed, and signals were made ordering them to return. His friend complied but Nelson, in the first of several famous acts of disobedience in his career, continued to advance on a seven-foot bear with his musket. The gun misfired, and the boy was about to attack with the butt of his weapon, when a cannon was fired from the ship, which caused the bear to make off before he could attack (and certainly kill) Nelson.

Brought before his angry captain, Nelson stood, lips thrust out, and answered the demand for an explanation: 'Sir, I wished to kill the bear, that I might carry its skin to my father.' That was all: a straightforward answer to a straightforward question. He was admonished and sent to his quarters.

As a voyage of exploration, the expedition was a failure, and its scientific findings were limited. But it had provided one more chapter in the long and essential book of experience for the midshipman.

From *Racehorse* to *Seahorse*. It was on board the frigate *Seahorse* over the next two years that the sailor was made, the boy became a man, and the resolution that made the hero was formed. Under the ship's commander, Captain George Farmer, Midshipman Nelson sailed to the Far East, witnessed strange sights and events, experienced the roaring forties, anchored at Trincomalee, and 'visited almost every part of the East Indies, from Bengal to Bussorah'.

At one time on this voyage Nelson was induced to sit down at the gaming table 'with a convivial East Indian party' and won £300, an immense sum of many thousands in today's currency. His amazement turned to horror when he later contemplated his situation if he had lost, and he vowed never to gamble again. Danger of another kind faced him many times in the foretop. And on one stirring day they raised a man-of-war flying the flag of one of France's allies. The *Seahorse* gave chase, caught up with the enemy, and opened fire. It was the first of many actions for Nelson, and he never forgot the moment when the enemy lowered her flag in surrender after more than a hundred rounds had been fired.

Nelson's life was never in great danger during this brief engagement. An eastern fever, a 'malignant disorder' which 'nearly baffled the power of medicine', brought him much closer to death. For weeks he tossed in his cot, sweating and becoming reduced almost to a skeleton. The surgeon saw that the only hope was to get him back to England, and in March 1776 he was found a berth in the *Dolphin*.

The seventeen-year-old boy had more feverish months in which to contemplate his fate. He saw little to encourage him, and recognized all too clearly 'the difficulties I had to surmount, and the little influence I possessed'. His useless life must soon end in failure. Depression overwhelmed the young man as the *Dolphin* slowly made her way across the Indian Ocean to the Cape of Good Hope, and thence across the Equator again into ever-colder northern seas.

Yet at one point on this voyage, a spiritual revelation opened up for Nelson, as if a consoling, healing hand had touched him and a voice had whispered of future fame. There is no doubt that an inspiration few people experience guided Nelson on his ascent to greatness. He was characteristically straightforward about it, and talked to his friends of 'the radiant orb' that beckoned him on. Of this first youthful revelation, he wrote that 'a sudden glow of patriotism was kindled within me, and presented my King and Country as my patron. My mind exulted in the idea. "Well, then," I exclaimed. "I will be a hero, and confiding in Providence, I will brave every . . . danger."'

An eighteenth-century view of Fort William in the Kingdom of Bengal, belonging to the East India Company.

A miniature believed to be Nelson as an adolescent.

Capt Horatio N
1781

2

Overture to Fame

The divine hand seemed to seize Nelson as he stepped ashore at Woolwich, where the *Dolphin* paid off on 4 September 1776. Uncle Maurice had been appointed Comptroller of the Navy. Already fit and strong again, Nelson found himself at once appointed acting lieutenant in the *Worcester*, a 64-gun ship of the line on convoy duties. War with the American colonies had broken out the previous year, and France seemed poised to intervene against Britain.

It was rough, hard work. 'I was at sea with convoys till 2 April 1777, and in very bad weather,' wrote Nelson. 'But although my age might have been a sufficient cause for not entrusting me with the charge of a Watch, yet Captain Robinson used to say "he felt as easy when I was upon deck, as any Officer in the Ship." '

The confidence was growing with the man. In April he took his examination for lieutenant. He had to face three officers, two post-captains and the Comptroller of the Navy, his uncle. At the satisfactory completion of the questions Suckling admitted the midshipman was his nephew and introduced him to the examiners.

'Why did you not, Sir, inform us of this relationship before the examination?' one of the captains asked.

'I did not wish the younker to be favoured. I felt convinced that he would pass a good examination; and you see, gentlemen, I have not been disappointed.'

Five days later, Nelson wrote to his older brother William, who was reading divinity at Christ College, Cambridge. Their father had just arrived in London, and he told William that he appeared to be in tolerable health. 'My sister and brother are both well, and desire their love to you.' He then told William of his success in his examination. 'So I am now left in the world to shift for myself, which I hope I shall do, so as to bring credit to myself and friends.'

There was time to sit for his portrait before he sailed away again,

Nelson aged eighteen painted by J. F. Rigaud. Nelson began sittings in 1777 before he sailed for the West Indies and the painting was finished in 1781 when Fort San Juan in Nicaragua was added in the background; he is wearing the uniform of a post-captain.

23

but not for its completion, which had to wait four years, by which time Nelson was a young captain. But John Rigaud's portrait already clearly reveals the youthful strength and confidence in the eighteen-year-old face.

A new ship, new responsibilities, and a new friend and ally. The ship was the frigate *Lowestoffe*, the responsibilities those of second lieutenant, under the command of Captain William Locker, a spritely, ruddy-complexioned, cheerful, kindly and utterly courageous officer of thirty-six years with much fighting behind him.

'Lay a Frenchman close and you will beat him,' Locker would instruct his young gentlemen, though he limped from a wound received while doing just that. This advocacy of close action with an enemy had a strong effect on Nelson. 'I have been your scholar,' he wrote to Locker many years later. 'It is you who taught me to board a Frenchman . . . and my sole merit in my profession is being a good scholar.'

French and American privateers were seriously damaging British trade in the West Indies. The *Lowestoffe* was to escort a convoy across the Atlantic, then search out and destroy them. After an uneventful crossing, the *Lowestoffe* sailed on her duties from Jamaica. Within a month she had claimed an American sloop, and another vessel soon after.

Prize money at last! The money awarded by the Admiralty Court to officers and men on the capture of an enemy ship and its cargo in time of war was one of the few attractions, and about the only inducement, to volunteer for this harsh and hazardous life at sea. It was, in fact, a driving force of immense power. The value was divided into eight parts, three to the captain, one to the commander-in-chief, one each to the officers and warrant officers, and two to be divided among the crew. Under favourable circumstances, it could lead to a fortune of tens of thousands for the captain, and for an ordinary seaman unheard-of riches of several hundred pounds.

This second capture was made in high seas, and the boat sent to seize the prize was in great danger.

'Have I no officer in this ship who can board the prize?' bawled Locker in the raging wind when the boat returned, rising and falling dizzily in the great seas.

Pushing aside the ship's master, Nelson leaped forward crying to him, 'It's my turn now, and if I come back it is yours.'

Nelson's boat was carried by the seas clear onto the decks of the

ABOVE Captain William Locker who became a lifelong friend of Nelson.

BELOW A sketch by Thomas Rowlandson showing naval agents quibbling about giving sailors their prize money.

RIGHT Nelson boarding a captured enemy ship during a gale, and in so doing earned valuable prize money for his ship, the *Lowestoffe*.

American, and was almost swamped. But he was able to take posses-sion, and the *Lowestoffe*'s company cheered for the youngster's courage, and their prize money.

For the next ten years, Nelson's career remained linked with the West Indies and the fighting against Spanish, French and American forces among the beautiful fever-infested islands and shores of Central America. Here he heard of the death of his Uncle Maurice,

and here he acquired a new patron, another new ally, in the Commander-in-Chief, Sir Peter Parker, who was quick to discern unusual qualities in the young lieutenant, and whose wife admired him, too.

Nelson's letters home tell of ships being cut out and taken, or lost; of a friend or a whole ship's crew down with the fever; of the arrival of great French forces and of the dread of being captured – 'I fear I shall have to learn French' – which was regarded as worse than a noble death in action.

Locker himself was forced to give up his command and return to England for health reasons. For the sake of posterity, that was an advantage. Nelson promised to write often to him, and did so, and the preserved letters tell us much of this period in Nelson's life. Locker had given him his first command, of the schooner *Little Lucy*, soon after his arrival. In her, 'I made myself a complete pilot', Nelson claimed, 'for all the passages through the islands on the north side of Hispaniola.'

Much of eighteenth-century naval action took place in the West Indies, protecting the important trade routes between the islands and England; this coloured engraving shows Rio Bueno in Jamaica.

26

There was a brief period in Parker's flagship as third lieutenant, with swift promotion to first lieutenant; then his first important command. In the brig *Badger* Nelson was dispatched 'to protect the "Mosquito shore", and the bay of Honduras, from the depredations of the American privateers'; a coastline that is now Costa Rica, Nicaragua, Honduras, Guatemala and the southern coastline of Mexico – a considerable responsibility for a single brig. The *Badger* made some prizes, and her commander was voted thanks by the colonists and traders.

Nelson was to remember 11 June 1779 with pleasure and pride all his life, for it was the day that marked the most important of all his promotions in the service. The captain of the frigate *Hinchingbrooke* had been killed in action, and Parker found himself with a vacancy for a post-captain. He did not hesitate. Nelson was informed, and was directed to assume command at once. He was not yet twenty-one, and under the long-established Admiralty regulations he was now certain – so long as he remained alive – of one day hoisting his flag as an admiral.

Six months later, in a letter to Locker, Nelson writes, 'I sailed in the *Hinchingbrooke* from Port Royal in the middle of September, to join the *Niger* and *Penelope*. We took four sail for which I shall share about £800 sterling.' There is news of the death by fever or in action of officers Locker had known on the station, and of more cheerful news: 'The *Salisbury* has brought in a Spanish storeship, mounting fifty-six guns, four hundred men, from Cadiz to Port Omoa, after a smart action of two hours and a-half. The *Salisbury* lost nine men; the Don fifty men.'

The same letter also informs his old commander of a new appointment: 'To go with an Expedition which is now on foot against the city of Grenada, upon the Lake of Nicaragua. How it will turn out, God knows.'

It turned out a triumph and a disaster. Spain was now at war with Britain, an ally of France and the rebellious American colonists. A blow at Spanish power, the mounting of an offensive, was decided upon in London – an amphibious attack against the Spanish settlements in Nicaragua. 'I was chosen to command the sea part of it,' wrote Nelson. He was to transport the military and naval forces to the mouth of the San Juan river, where they were to force their way to a Spanish fort and invest it.

In the event, Nelson's responsibilities did not end here. The army commander described how 'a light-haired boy came to me in a little frigate. In two or three days he displayed himself, and afterwards he directed all the operations.'

This 'light-haired boy', this self-confident naval post-captain, discovered that no one had ever been up the river, 'none but Spaniards since the time of the buccaneers'. There were no charts. No one knew where the fort was situated.

'Major Polson, who commanded the soldiers, will tell you of my exertions: how I quitted my Ship and carried troops in boats one hundred miles up a river . . . It will then be told', Nelson recounted with engaging conceit and honesty, 'how I boarded (if I may be allowed the expression) an outpost of the Enemy, situated on an Island in the river; that I made batteries, and afterwards fought them, and was a principal cause of our success.'

BELOW The Hon. William 'Blue Billy' Cornwallis, later to become an Admiral, who was a friend of Nelson in the West Indies.

All true. But the price paid for the capture and temporary possession of this fort was terrible. 'Yellow Jack' fever struck the ill-equipped expedition. The jungle was heavy with infected insects and poisonous snakes, and the men fell in hundreds. When Nelson was ordered to return prematurely with his ship's company to take over a new command, 'with a complement of two hundred men, eighty-seven took to their beds in one night; and of the two hundred, one hundred and forty-five were buried.' Of another ship's company, no more than ten survived.

Nelson, inevitably, was struck down too, and his life was saved only by the most tender and diligent nursing by a notable negress, a one-time slave called Cuba Cornwallis, who assumed this name after the naval captain who had obtained her freedom. As soon as he could be moved, he stayed with the Parkers. His recovery was so slow and incomplete that he decided he must return to England for a spell. The Hon. William 'Blue Billy' Cornwallis himself commanded the ship in which he made the voyage, and like the woman he had freed from slavery, nursed him all the way home: 'his care and attention saved my life'.

A winter in Bath, where his father often came to escape the bitter north-easterlies of Burnham Thorpe. 'My health is very nearly perfectly restored', he could report by February 1781. Some time in London, staying with Suckling's brother, William, of the Customs and Navy Office. Then beloved Burnham in the early summer, spending much time with his sisters and brothers. He loved them

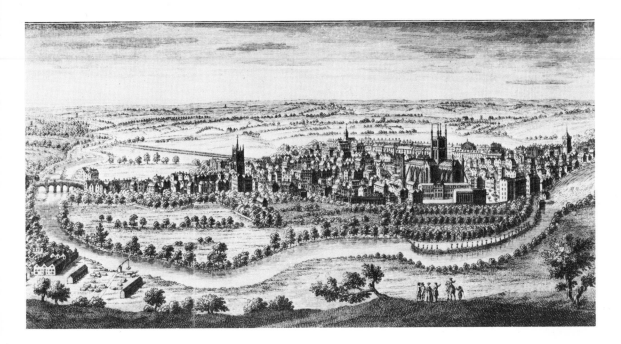

ABOVE A view of the elegant city of Bath in the late eighteenth century.

all – William the curate, Edmund the accountant, Suckling the draper's apprentice, Susannah married and living in nearby Wells, and the others – and did all he could to see them happy and secure, now and later when he became so famous.

But he remained anxious about his health. There was a strong strain of the hypochondriac in Horatio Nelson, but as so often happens, there was justification for it. His letters are often much concerned with his health; and now it was of a sense of paralysis in his limbs. Of his left arm, 'From the shoulder to my fingers' ends are as half dead; but the Surgeon and Doctors give me hopes it will all go off . . .'

In August 1781 the news of an appointment cheered him up. The *Albemarle* was a 28-gun frigate, the better for being a French prize as the French were the better designers. A winter of convoy work in the North Sea did not improve his health, or lessen his anxiety about it, especially when his ship was ordered to North America.

In the event, he found the North American climate restored him to robust health. Quebec was his destination, a convoy to be escorted there, its cargo including bullion of a hundred thousand pounds. 'Health, that greatest of blessings, is what I never truly enjoyed till I saw *Fair* Canada. The change it has wrought, I am convinced, is truly wonderful,' he wrote to his father.

C. Mosley Sculp.

1
Early one Morn a Jolly brisk Tarr
Signal being made for Sailing
Nimbly stept down & told his Dear
Who was her loss bevailing
Orders are come we must Unmoor
The Boat long side lays waiting
Haste away Moll you must on Shore
This is no time for prating.

2
Molly with Arms about his Neck
Look'd as if Life had left her
So sad a word from her dear Jack
Of Spirits quite bereft her
He seing her Cheeks to look so wan
Laugh'd at the silly Creature
Till from her Heart the Blood began
To brighten every Feature.

The
SAILOR'S FAREWELL

3
Prithee my Dear since I must go
Why such concern at parting
You may be happy you well know
Other Mens Wives concerting
Oh wo my Dear say no such thing
Should Fear cease from crying
I should perhaps rejoice & Sing
If you by a Shot lay Dying.

4
Just as she spoke old Trunules Call
All hands aloft did rattle
Jack with a frown crys Zounscome Moll
This is no time for Prattle
Into the Boat the Ships on may
Molly climbs slowly over
At every step she crys day day
And Sighs do her Fear discover

5
Now afar off with watry Eyes
She saw the Ship a Sailing
Shither she looks & there she Cries
Speech o'er her Fears prevailing
Oh there he goes my Dear is gone
Gone is my Hearts desire
Oh may the Bullets Miss my John
That is all I require.

Printed for Carington Bowles in S.t Paul. Church Yard London

17

Not only did Nelson's health prosper in Canada. His love life briefly flourished, and – not for the last time – almost got out of hand. In Quebec he fell madly in love with the highly attractive daughter of the Provost-Marshal. The fact that she was only sixteen in no way deterred him. On a crisp autumn day in October, when his ship was due to go down the river, he was seen by a friend returning to the landing stage and then walking purposefully along it. What are you doing, Horatio? the friend asked anxiously. Why are you returning? I am in love, I cannot depart; I am asking for her hand, I shall leave the service. The friend protested. You cannot end your fine career for a girl you hardly know! There was a violent argument. And then, crestfallen at his defeat (but realistic, too), the post-captain re-embarked in his boat and returned to his ship, his heart broken.

Six days later the *Albemarle* dropped anchor near Sandy Hook lighthouse, south of Manhattan Island and New York. 'I found Lord Hood here upon my arrival, and I have requested him to take me with him to the West Indies,' Nelson wrote home. It seemed that the admiral, fresh from the great victory of the Battle of the Saints off Dominica against Count François de Grasse, honoured Nelson highly by a letter, 'for wishing', according to Nelson, 'to go off this

Station, to a Station of Service, and has promised me his friendship. Prince William is with him . . .'

Between these lines one can detect the eager, ambitious young captain swiftly 'making his number' with the Commander-in-Chief, charming him and impressing him with his confident style and articulate conversation. Here, in this man-of-war, were two men of power and privilege who, Nelson quickly discerned, could be of immense value to him.

Prince William, the future Duke of Clarence and King William IV, was still only a raw midshipman. But not only was he to become one more friend; the Prince had a keen, discerning eye, and has given us a sharp word picture of Nelson at this time, long before his greatness:

> When Captain Nelson . . . came in his barge alongside, he appeared to be the merest boy of a Captain I ever beheld: and his dress was worthy of attention. He had on a full laced uniform; his lank unpowdered hair was tied in a stiff Hessian tail, of an extraordinary length; the old-fashioned flaps of his waistcoat added to the general quaintness of his figure, and produced an appearance which particularly attracted my notice; for I had never seen anything like it before, nor could I imagine who he was, nor what he came about.

Then Lord Hood introduced the future hero to the future King of England; and the young prince decided:

> There was something irresistibly pleasing in his address and conversation; and an enthusiasm, when speaking on professional subjects that showed he was no common being.

By now, the American War of Independence was fading out, and with it any opportunity for Nelson to acquire fame and substantial prize money. The *Albemarle* did capture one French vessel which, he judged, 'will clear upward of £20,000', but the prize was made with the rest of the fleet in sight which, by a technicality, meant a share-out so wide that his portion was very modest. Then there was the affair of Turks Island, shortly before peace was declared with France. Underestimating the strength of the French garrison in an attempt to capture this French stronghold in the Bahamas, the landing party was driven off.

Nelson brought the *Albemarle* into Portsmouth harbour on 26 June 1783, and paid off the frigate. The benefits of his contact with the admiral and the prince at New York were soon made

ABOVE Prince William, the third son of George III, as a young midshipman.
FACING PAGE ABOVE The surrender of the British army to General Washington at Yorktown in 1781.

FACING PAGE BELOW An English frigate with four captured American merchant-men anchored off the American coastline; painted by Francis Holman in 1778.

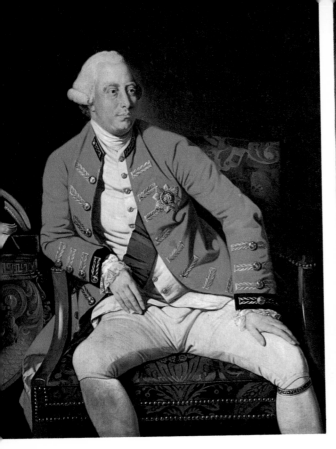

evident. Three weeks later he was at a Royal *levée* at St James's Palace in company with Lord Hood. It was his first meeting with his sovereign, George III, who invited him to stay at Windsor Castle in order to meet Prince William again, and see him off on the Grand Tour he was about to undertake. The King saw Nelson through his rise to fame and all his days of glory. George III's life began twenty years before Nelson's, and extended another fifteen years after his death.

His admiration for this naval officer began with these summer meetings. As far as Nelson's private life was concerned, however, George III was to have very different feelings, as Nelson was to discover to his cost.

A flirtation with politics, a flirtation with a Miss Andrews, occupied Nelson during the first months after his return to a country in a rare state of peace with France and Spain. Late in 1783 Nelson had determined to visit the land of his one-time enemies, and crossed the Channel to Calais, with the intention of learning the language and doing a Grand Tour in humble miniature. He expressed little admiration for the country, found it dirty and inefficient; and when

ABOVE LEFT George III, painted by Johann Zoffany in 1771.
ABOVE RIGHT Admiral Lord Hood painted by Sir Joshua Reynolds in 1783.

he fell in love (it was bound to happen again soon), it was to an
English girl with a brother in the Royal Navy.

Once more, it was a fiery, brief affair. He desperately wanted to
marry this Miss Andrews, but because he had no fortune and a tiny
half-pay income, he wrote to William Suckling, the one man who
might help him – 'Will you, if I should marry, allow me a hundred a
year? . . . Life is not worth preserving without happiness . . .'

The uncle proved generous, the lady unwilling. Thwarted, Nelson
returned home. His naval luck was better. The Irish peer and admiral, Richard Howe, was First Sea Lord. His career had been
notable. Like Nelson, he had been promoted post-captain at the age
of twenty, and had fought valiantly and successfully in the War of
Austrian Succession, and the Seven Years' War which had followed
it. The 'Glorious First of June' was his greatest victory. With his
keen nose for exceptional talent, he was prepared to offer Nelson a
peacetime command of some responsibility. The *Boreas* was a 28-
gun frigate that was ordered to proceed to the West Indies with an
assortment of midshipmen, Nelson's brother William, who had
determined to become a naval chaplain (against Horatio's advice),
the Commander-in-Chief's wife, their daughter and so much bag-

35

gage and equipment that Nelson complained that he would be 'pretty well filled with *lumber*' as well as 'the eternal clack' of his commander's wife.

The voyage was uncomfortable, the commission not a success. Nelson, like so many men of war in the role of a man of peace, was not always a success. Now that the war was over in the Caribbean, the arm of diplomacy had succeeded the arm of the sword, and the position in the West Indies was a delicate one. Much of the trade was American, and the traders themselves, once privileged British colonists, had now become foreigners. The Navigation Act, which vessels of the West Indies fleet were supposed to uphold, forbade *any* foreign trade.

Bribery and corruption among the producers, shippers and men of commerce saw to it that trade continued as profitably as ever. When Nelson, in the course of what he regarded as his duty, began to interfere with this trade, to halt and take into custody these American trading vessels, he at once aroused resentment among the rich commercial gentlemen in Jamaica. Like so many officers who had grown up within the enclosed life of the service, Nelson failed to recognize the wickedness of the commercial world outside, where, it seemed, greed and gain took precedence above duty and patriotism.

Everybody, Nelson discovered, was up to their neck in corruption that was lining the purses of the planters, merchants and customs officers of the islands, on the one hand, and the American commercial interests and masters and crew of merchantmen on the other. Even his Commander-in-Chief, Sir Richard Hughes, was involved. 'His easy temper had made him the dupe of some artful people,' commented Nelson at first, in an effort to find some excuse for such dishonesty in a naval officer.

Later, however, when Nelson insisted on following the letter of the law, when he turned back American trading vessels, when he ordered them to leave with their illicit cargoes half unloaded, he was ordered by Admiral Hughes not to interfere. Nelson, socially ostracized wherever he sailed, appealed to the Admiralty and the Secretary of State in London, and even addressed a humble memorial to the King. When he protested to Governor Shirley of the Leeward Islands at this encouragement to illegality, he was told peremptorily, 'Old Generals are not in the habit of taking advice from young gentlemen.'

The CRUEL TREATMENT of
THE SLAVES
in the
WEST-INDIES

ABOVE This engraving shows the cruel treatment of slaves in the West Indies by the planters who are driving them from the ship to work in the plantations.

BELOW The thriving West India Docks in London show the importance of trade with the Caribbean, mostly in sugar and in rum; the vital task of protecting these trade routes lay with the Royal Navy.

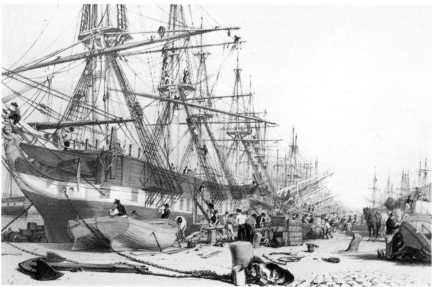

Spiritedly, Nelson replied, 'I have the honour, Sir, of being as old as the Prime Minister of England, and think myself as capable of commanding one of His Majesty's Ships as that Minister [Pitt] is of governing the State.'

At length, Nelson found himself sued for assault and imprisonment when he seized four American merchantmen who had ignored his orders to leave Nevis roads within forty-eight hours. He was forced to remain on board the *Boreas* for eight weeks until a judge upheld the seizures. Later, the Admiralty paid Nelson the costs of his defence.

Nelson wrote to Locker on 15 January 1785, 'You will believe that I am not very popular with the people. They have never visited me, and I have not set foot in any private house since I have been on the Station, and all for doing my duty by being *true to the interests of Great Britain* . . .'

Six months later, however, he had visited at least one house on the island of Nevis. There are two glimpses of Nelson on this island at this time that add further shadings to the complex and sometimes seemingly contradictory picture of the twenty-seven-year-old naval captain. The first comes from the widowed President of the island, John Richardson Herbert, who came down early one morning to

FACING PAGE A view of Port Royal and Kingston Harbour in Jamaica, an engraving in 1782.
INSET Nelson sketched by Cuthbert Colling-wood in 1784; he is wearing a wig, having temporarily lost his hair due to illness.
RIGHT The island of Nevis.

find Nelson, 'that great little man of whom everyone is so afraid, playing in the next room, under the dining table, with Mrs Nisbet's child'. The next comes from a letter written to this Mrs Nisbet from another woman:

> We have at last seen the Captain of the *Boreas* [she writes]. He came up just before dinner, much heated, and was very silent; yet seemed, accord-ing to the old adage, to think the more. He declined drinking any wine; but after dinner, when the President, as usual, gave the following toasts, 'the King', 'the Queen and Royal Family', and 'Lord Hood', this strange man regularly filled his glass, and observed that those were always bumper toasts with him; which having drank, he uniformly passed the bottle, and relapsed into his former taciturnity. . . . If you, Fanny, had been there, we think you would have made something of him; for you have been in the habit of attending to these odd sort of people. . . .

This proved to be the case, and soon Nelson met this widowed Mrs Frances Nisbet, mother to the boy Josiah with whom he had been

caught playing under the table, and was writing home to his father about her.

Fanny, fine of feature, sweet and gentle of nature, with a complexion carefully protected from the tropical sun, had been briefly married to a doctor. Widowed and without means, this intelligent, well-spoken (and fluent in French) young woman who was a few months older than Nelson, had been invited to the island, where her father was senior judge and her uncle President. Here she 'did the flowers', acted as hostess and brought up her little boy.

Nelson paid court to the widow with characteristic zeal and single-mindedness, seeing in this attractive woman a compound of wife and mother to fill the yearning that had so often been frustrated in the past. Within a few weeks he proposed, and was accepted. The father, too, capitulated – 'lowered his colours' Nelson might have said – and Nelson wrote to Uncle William Suckling that he 'is very rich and proud . . . I have lived at his house, when at Nevis, since June last and am a great favourite of his. I have told him I am as poor as Job; but he tells me he likes me, and I am descended from a good family, which his pride likes.'

By this time – towards the end of 1786 – for Nelson life had taken on a new colour. He was passionately in love. ('Separated from you, what pleasure can I feel? None, be assured: all my happiness is centred with thee.') He was temporary Commander-in-Chief, the dishonourable Hughes having sailed for home. And Prince William Henry, now a post-captain commanding HMS *Pegasus*, was serving under him, and had agreed to act as best man at his wedding.

The prince fulfilled his promise on 11 March 1787 when the couple were married at Nevis. Nelson wrote a letter to Locker recounting some of the troubles he had experienced in the West Indies during this difficult commission. 'But let me lay a balance on the other side – I am married to an amiable woman, that far makes amends for everything: indeed till I married her I never knew happiness. And I am morally certain she will continue to make me a happy man for the rest of my days.'

If only that could have been true, life would have been smoother for the hero. And, perhaps, we should have been left with a less puzzling, fascinating and multi-coloured sailor to remember.

Frances Nisbet, later to become Nelson's wife.

Nelson never served another commission in peacetime. For the rest of his life, he was to know only boredom ashore, and war.

To spend the next five years of his life with his newly married wife, mostly in his beloved Norfolk, might have seemed paradise to many naval officers after a long and difficult commission abroad. It is true that he had a strong feeling for country life, a romantic conception of tilling the soil and observing the turn of the seasons and nature's round. He also enjoyed introducing Fanny to Norfolk and to his neighbours and friends. Though poor on his half-pay of some £50 a year, and the £100 allowance he and Fanny each received, money was not the first problem. The trouble lay deeper than that. It lay in restlessness and frustration. It was many years now since he had lain weak and sick on board the *Dolphin* and determined to be a hero. That, he had convinced himself, was to be his destiny: heroic, triumphant, the saviour of his nation and a humble servant of his Sovereign. 'The radiant orb' had beckoned him on then. And where had it led him? To a parsonage, helping his father to farm the glebe land, helping his wife to bring up her son.

Nelson used every device to get himself a ship, 'even a boat, to serve my Country, but in vain; there was a prejudice at the Admiralty evidently against me, which I can neither guess at, or in the least account for.' We can make a shrewd guess at the reason for this neglect. However correct and dutiful Nelson had been on his last commission, it had led to many troubles for the Admiralty, and Nelson himself had made enemies.

Lord Hood was now at the Admiralty. There is no doubt that this admiral had been struck by the wartime qualities of the young post-captain. He was to show his trust in him again, as a fighting sailor. When Nelson was asked outright by Prince William Henry, now the Duke of Clarence, how he stood with Hood, Nelson replied, 'I can readily and truly answer. We have not for a long time had any communication with each other . . . I certainly cannot look on Lord Hood as my friend; but I have the satisfaction of knowing that I never gave his Lordship just cause to be my enemy.'

Once a year, Nelson had made the long and expensive pilgrimage to the Admiralty in London to enquire if there was any employment for him; returning weary and depressed days later.

Nelson's return to the sea and to the war service that was to initiate the stirring events marked by the stars of his heroic actions, coincided with the execution of King Louis XVI in the Place de la Révolution in Paris. Soon two figures were to emerge

Louis XVI was guillo-
tined in Paris on
21 January 1793 in
front of large crowds
in the Place de la
Révolution, now the
Place de la Concorde.

from the holocaust and bloodshed: Napoleon, who was to conquer most of Europe and nearly reach Moscow in the east and the Nile in the south; and Nelson, who was to frustrate this soldier at sea, destroy his fleets, and help bring about his downfall ten years after his own death in action.

At the beginning of 1793 Napoleon was an obscure twenty-three-year-old officer in the French army, and Nelson's reputation was known only to a small number of professionals. But the destinies of these two men – the soldier who did not understand the meaning and importance of sea power, and the sailor who was unsuccessful in his land actions – were now to become inextricably linked.

3

'I Got a Little Hurt this Morning'

In his *Sketch of My Life,* Nelson wrote, 'On the 30th of January 1793 I was commissioned in the very handsomest way for the *Agamemnon,* 64; and was put under the command of that great man and excellent officer, Lord Hood.' War would be declared within days, and the two men were friends again.

A ship of the line, a battleship. 'After clouds comes sunshine', Nelson wrote to Fanny from London in transports of relief and joy. 'The Admiralty so smile upon me, that really I am as much surprised as when they frowned.' But we can also see Mrs Nelson reading this letter with anxiety in her heart. She easily became fretful, and later in this letter she read that 'Everything indicates War'.

Nelson chose his officers with care, his boatswain from the *Boreas* ('one of the best boatswains I have seen in His Majesty's service'), and among the 'young gentlemen' – the midshipmen – was his stepson Josiah and a distant cousin, young Maurice Suckling.

On the way out to the Mediterranean, where the *Agamemnon* was to serve under Hood, Nelson worked up his ship to a keen degree of efficiency, especially the gunnery. Rapid rather than accurate fire was the secret of success in naval battles that were fought at a maximum range of four or five hundred yards, and usually much closer. Nelson had no time for gun-aiming; by his reckoning a ship should be so close that the broadside could not fail to make a hit. A well-trained British gun crew was capable of firing a round every ninety seconds, or even, very briefly, a round a minute; and in a first-class gunnery ship the guns would be fired in a continuous ripple from forward to aft, one crew firing a few seconds after their neighbour in order to reduce the concussive shock to the ship's hull.

Nelson being wounded in the arm during the attack on Santa Cruz, Tenerife, 24 July 1797.

45

By August, the *Agamemnon* and the rest of Hood's fleet was in the Mediterranean and off Toulon, the French naval base that had not succumbed to revolution and was being used by France's enemies as a centre for counter-revolution. Lord Hood was already landing armed parties to reinforce the defenders of the city, who included troops from Sardinia, Spain and Britain. But the need for further strength against the pressing revolutionary forces was urgent. They could be obtained rapidly only from the independent Kingdom of Naples and the Two Sicilies, which was traditionally friendly to Britain. To persuade the Neapolitans to dispatch a substantial force would require diplomacy.

For this delicate but critically important task Hood selected Nelson from among his captains. His decision was to have far-reaching consequences on Nelson's future career, both professionally and personally.

Nelson first set eyes on Emma Hamilton in Naples on a September evening in 1793. Fanny's first news of the woman she was to learn to detest was in a few lines of a letter her husband wrote to her from Naples on 14 September, informing her that the wife of the British Minister in Naples had been 'wonderfully kind and good to Josiah. She is a young woman of amiable manner', he continued, 'and who does honour to the station to which she is raised.'

The elevation of her station to which Nelson refers related to the well-known fact that this plump, luscious, vital, intelligent and ambitious thirty-two-year-old woman had been born of humble parents in Cheshire and had risen to marry Sir William Hamilton, a grand, rich and elderly collector and aesthete, and now British

View of the naval base of Toulon after its recapture from the English and Spaniards in December 1793, a gouache by Honoré de Balzac.

FACING PAGE *Sir William Hamilton as a Knight of the Bath*, painted by David Allan in 1775; the painting, with Vesuvius in the background, pays tribute to his acknowledged expertise on the volcanoes of Naples and Sicily and also to his important collections of antique Greek and Roman vases.

ABOVE Emma's mother, known as Mrs Cadogan.

Ambassador at the Neapolitan court, by way of notorious affairs with men in society. Her mother, recognizing early the tempting promise of her attractive daughter, took her to London from the country, and she made rapid progress as a courtesan in the best eighteenth-century French style. Artists of the calibre of Sir Thomas Lawrence and John Hoppner painted her, and George Romney fell head-over-heels in love with his model, whom he idealized in one of the best-known portraits.

Emma's mother became 'Mrs Cadogan', a housekeeper and companion in the household to which Emma was attached. Emma was at length 'given' by Charles Greville to his uncle, Sir William Hamilton, who took her out to Naples as his mistress, with her mother still in attendance. Here she became a prominent social figure and political intriguer, and persuaded Hamilton to marry her. She thus became at one stroke no longer quite disreputable, and Lady Hamilton.

Like most sailors, Nelson's marriage vows were left behind at Gibraltar (as the saying went), and he had affairs ashore when opportunity offered. But on this occasion there was nothing more

FACING PAGE *Lady Hamilton as Circe*, painted by George Romney.
RIGHT A drawing by Frederick Rehburg showing one of Emma's Attitudes, her representations of classical and other figures, which soon made her famous in Naples.
OVERLEAF *Lady Hamilton as a Bacchante*, a miniature by Henry Bone after Madame Vigée-le-Brun.

than the registering of the attractions of 'the divine Emma', as she became known on this first visit to Naples.

Diplomatically, Nelson's visit was completely successful. King Ferdinand enthusiastically complied with the request for troops to support the allies at Toulon, before the *Agamemnon* was forced to make a hasty departure from the port on news of a French corvette being at sea and close to hand. Nelson's pursuit of the enemy was unsuccessful. An action with five French ships smaller than his own three-decker was equally abortive, Nelson being forced to break off the fight due to damage to his masts and rigging. 'The Nelson touch' had not yet evidenced itself.

There was further disappointment and chagrin in December 1793 when it became clear that, for all their efforts to defend it, the important port of Toulon was doomed to fall – thanks in large measure to the efforts of a young artillery officer, Lieutenant-Colonel Bonaparte. 'Lord Hood attempted to rally the flying troops, but it was impossible,' Nelson wrote to his father. 'Then began a scene of horror which may be conceived, not described. The mob rose; death called forth all its myrmidons, which destroyed the miserable inhabitants in the shape of swords, pistols, fire and water.' The holocaust he witnessed further hardened Nelson's opinion of the French as a brutal and ruthless race from whom his country must be protected at all costs.

The loss of Toulon meant that the British fleet must find a new base from which to carry on the struggle, and the blockade of the French. Corsica appeared to provide the best hope, an island on which the fiercely nationalist inhabitants were already in revolt against the occupying French forces. Nelson took a prominent part in the successful struggle, in uneasy alliance with the Corsicans, against the French, all through that burning hot summer. It was arduous, unrewarding work ashore, with greater danger from disease than from the enemy.

But it was an enemy shell that inflicted the first of three disabling wounds on Nelson, long before he had become the heroic crippled figure of his years of triumph. While inspecting the batteries at Calvi, a shell exploded on the breastwork nearby, throwing splinters, dirt and stones into his face. His friend, Tom Fremantle, was with him and described how Nelson was thrown to the ground, covered in dust and blood.

The young Napoleon Bonaparte, who was soon to become the leader of France in the war against England, on board *L'Orient* in 1798 when he was aged twenty-eight, a miniature painted by André Dutertre.

When the surgeon cleaned him up, he saw a deep wound above the right eye. Nelson at first treated the matter lightly. 'I got a little hurt this morning: not much, as you may judge from my writing.' He could distinguish light from dark, and hoped to recover the use of his sight. 'It confined me one day, when, thank God, I was enabled to attend to my duty.'

The eye did not improve, however. Six months later he was writing home to Fanny, telling her that it 'is grown worse, and is in almost total darkness, and very painful at times; but never mind, I can see very well with the other.'

He was not even to be spared pain from the other eye. Especially in the glare of the Mediterranean sun, his surviving eye ached from the strain of working for both. He was later forced to wear a shade above it. (The traditional picture of the hero wearing a patch over his right, sightless eye is inaccurate.)

53

Again, and not for the last time, a land campaign had brought Nelson ill luck. That the fates linked his fighting fortunes with the sea rather than with the land was shown – but still only in a modest way – on 13 March 1794, after a winter of frustration and a period at Leghorn to rest his men and refit his ship. Nelson was serving now under Admiral Lord Hotham, an amiable sailor of modest accomplishment. Nelson considered him 'not intended by nature for a Commander-in-Chief, which requires a man of more active a turn of mind'.

Early in the month, intelligence reached Leghorn that the French fleet of seventeen ships had put to sea from Toulon with the intention of recovering Corsica. Hotham left harbour with fourteen ships, including the *Agamemnon*. In spite of their superior strength, the French fled soon after sighting the English fleet, and the *Agamemnon*, being a fast sailor and well manned (though undermanned), was the first to catch up and engage the rearmost ship, the bigger *Ça Ira*.

Almost at once, Nelson's high standard of gunnery began to tell. The Frenchman was holed again and again, and lost a hundred dead, against a handful of wounded in the *Agamemnon*. The next morning, the *Ça Ira* struck her colours, and Nelson put one of his lieutenants on board. It was his first great prize, signifying the preface to his ever-growing saga of victories.

Nelson was not in the least satisfied. Hotham had taken only one other Frenchman, and when Nelson proposed that they should continue the pursuit he received the un-Nelsonian and exasperating signal, 'We must be contented. We have done very well.'

In a *cri de coeur* to Fanny, Nelson wrote, 'Now, had we taken ten sail, and allowed the eleventh to escape, when it would have been possible to have got at her, I could never have called it well done. We should have had such a day as, I believe, the annals of England ever produced.' And then, with simple truth: 'I wish to be Admiral, and in command of the English fleet.'

We move on now to 19 January 1796, and the first chapter of great events. Once again it is an encounter with a man destined to be a friend and ally that ensures the success to which Nelson so ardently aspired.

In his long life John Jervis, later 1st Earl of St Vincent, stood for all that was great in eighteenth-century British naval history. Like

ABOVE Admiral Sir John Jervis.
BELOW The territorial

Nelson, Jervis had first gone to sea at a tender age. Soon the career of this beefy, brilliant, handsome and utterly courageous sailor was like a victory roll of British naval achievement. As a post-captain at the capture of Quebec he heard from Wolfe's own lips the General's last whispered message to his betrothed. He once captured a more powerful French ship of the line without losing a single man, suffering himself only two black eyes, and was awarded a baronetcy. He later led a successful expedition that resulted in the capture of vital French possessions in the Caribbean. His meeting with Nelson was to lead to his own greatest victories, too.

The *Agamemnon* was worn out, destined only to make a hazardous passage home for a refit – 'poor old *Agamemnon!*' – and on 11 June 1796 Nelson hoisted his Commodore's broad pendant on board the two-decker *Captain,* 74. She was an appropriately named man-of-war. Two months later he appointed his own first flag-captain. His name was Ralph Willett Miller, and he was to become one of Nelson's most loyal friends and subordinates, one of his famed 'Band of Brothers'. Already these were growing in numbers. Since the San Juan expedition he had formed a lasting and close friendship with Cuthbert Collingwood, a dour, steady Newcastle man, the complete antithesis of Nelson in character and appearance but a marvellous foil to his fiery genius. Besides Tom Fremantle, there was Thomas Hardy, still only a lieutenant. In a gallant effort to rescue one of his own men overboard close to a

rivalry between France and England, a cartoon by Gillray.

Spanish ship, Hardy had lowered a jolly boat which was swept on a current towards the enemy. 'By God, I'll not lose Hardy!' Nelson had exclaimed, and ordered his mizzen-topsail to be backed. The Spaniards thought he was spoiling for a fight against impossible odds, hesitated – and Hardy was rescued.

It was a time for this sort of comradeship and accord in the Royal Navy, for 1796 was a dark year for Britain. The artillery officer of the Toulon siege had become the dictator Napoleon Bonaparte, who now swept all before him on land, intent on conquering the world. In October Spain declared war on Britain, and the following month the Royal Navy was forced to withdraw entirely from the Mediterranean. The British economy was in a bad way, the banks had suspended payments, there was talk of invasion from France. By the end of the year the need for a victory to sustain British spirits had become urgent.

The preliminaries to Nelson's first major fleet action began on a

damp misty day in February 1797, when he sighted a number of scattered Spanish men-of-war. They were units of the Spanish fleet, twenty-seven ships of the line in all, that were attempting to break through from Cartagena in the Mediterranean to rendezvous at Brest on the French Atlantic coast with the Dutch and French fleets preparatory to the invasion and conquest of Britain.

The Spaniards had broken through the Strait of Gibraltar, and had then been driven far out into the Atlantic by a strong easterly wind. They were heading now for Cadiz before intending to proceed north to Brest. Jervis was off Cape St Vincent, ready for them, but able to muster only fifteen ships of the line. The Spanish fleet, commanded by the notable Admiral Don José de Córdova, was sighted by Jervis's fleet early on the morning of 14 February 1797. The big ships appeared one by one out of the dawn mist, their position and numbers being reported by signal flags from Jervis's alert and experienced scouting frigate captains. These signals were read and passed to Robert Calder, Captain of the Fleet, and thence to Jervis himself: sixty-two years old now, tough as salt beef and relishing the prospect of a great battle.

'There are eight sail of the line, Sir John,' Calder reported.

The north view of Gibraltar in 1791; Gibraltar was a strategic base for the Royal Navy in the Mediterranean.

A view of the victory of the Battle of Cape St Vincent, 15 February 1797, painted by Robert Dodd.

'Very well, Sir,' replied Jervis, surveying his own fifteen.

'There are twenty sail of the line, Sir John.'

'Very well, Sir.'

A few minutes later, as most Spanish masts emerged from the murk, tossing and heaving in the heavy seas: 'There are twenty-five sail of the line, Sir John.'

'Very well, Sir.'

'There are twenty-seven sail of the line, Sir John.'

'Enough, Sir,' snapped Jervis. 'No more of that. The die is cast, and if there are fifty I will go through them.'

The Spanish fleet was sailing on a westerly heading in two main but scattered groups, and with a strong wind from the south-west. Jervis and Nelson, and every British captain, had complete confidence in their ships and their men, and in their ability to strike a damaging blow at the enemy. The poor station keeping and the evident lack of resolution of the enemy added to their self-assurance. However, Nelson knew as well as Jervis that, with odds at almost two-to-one, a slogging gun duel could well prove fatal to the British.

As the British line bore down on Córdova, the Spanish admiral

57

recognized that he would never be able to unite his two divisions, and brought his own, westerly, division round onto a northerly heading with the intention of passing astern of the enemy. Escape was all he asked for.

It was midday now; St Valentine's Day. Was that a good augury? All but one 112-gun ship of the easterly, or leeward, Spanish division was scattering in apparent panic, and Jervis recognized the danger of losing the enemy altogether under these difficult conditions. Minutes now counted, and at 12.08 precisely, Jervis's flagship *Victory* ran up the signal for the line to tack in succession through 180 degrees, reversing course and engaging the rear of the enemy.

The leading British ship was the *Culloden*, commanded by another great sailor destined to become one more of Nelson's Band of Brothers. Tom Troubridge, an Irishman born in London (he always spoke in a heavy brogue), was a contemporary of Nelson's and had served with him on board the *Seahorse* many years before.

As Troubridge ordered, 'Break the stop – down with the helm!' and the *Culloden* swung round on the opposite tack, Jervis watched him with satisfaction from the quarterdeck of the *Victory*. 'Look at Troubridge there', he is reported as calling out. 'He tacks his ship in battle as if the eyes of England were upon him. And would to God they were,' he added, 'for they would see him to be what I know him to be – and, by Heaven, Sir, as the Dons will soon feel him to be.'

Already Jervis's flagship had terribly punished the Spanish 112 from the easterly division, which had shown a less urgent need to flee than his consorts and received two devastating broadsides. 'He appeared to be in great confusion', reported the *Victory*'s log; but not so much confusion that the Spanish ship could not get in a broadside, one shot of which took away the foresail yard of the *Colossus*, which was forced out of line, and out of the engagement altogether.

The battle was now becoming very hot as the Spanish rearguard was closed upon by the British vanguard. Jervis himself, on his quarterdeck and with the Spanish shot and bullets on all sides of him, was finding it difficult to distinguish friend from foe in the smoke and confusion, and to assess the progress of the battle. Suddenly he found his face and chest covered with blood, tissue and brains.

The captain of marines rushed up, fearing that he was mortally

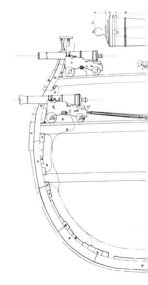

ABOVE Rear-Admiral Sir Thomas Troubridge, Nelson's friend for many years. BELOW A midship section of an eighteenth-century ship showing the position of the cannon.

wounded. 'I'm not at all hurt', Jervis replied, wiping from his face the remains of a marine beside him whose head had been knocked off, 'but do, George, try if you can get me an orange.' A midshipman did so, and as soon as the admiral had rinsed his mouth he ordered the signal to be hoisted to engage the enemy more closely.

It was now one o'clock. The fleets had been in contact for over an hour. But only a small proportion of the ships of both sides had given or taken punishment. Nelson's *Captain* was one of those ships that had not yet fired a shot. And, clear of the smoke of battle, the Commodore judged that Córdova's plan to bring the greater number of his ships astern of the British line, and thus effect their escape, might well succeed. The consequences of the Spaniards making Cadiz, and eventually Brest, could be fatal to Britain. Besides, to be inactive in the midst of a great battle was more than Nelson could stand.

In his first fleet engagement, and for the first of several times in his life, Nelson now made a decision that was to turn the tide of battle, and shape the course of history. Jervis had timed his turn too late, and the only way to correct the situation was for Nelson to grasp the initiative himself. In defiance of Jervis's signal, and of the sacred Royal Navy *Fighting Instructions*, Nelson ordered the *Captain* to wear out of the line and stand on the other tack: in effect, to take a short cut to the Spanish vanguard sailing in the opposite direction, and to battle. Also without orders, Collingwood in the *Excellent*, and last in the line, followed his commodore and friend.

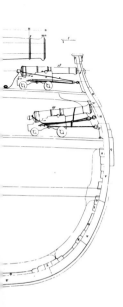

Almost at once Nelson found himself engaged with the *Santissima Trinidad*, a four-decker and the biggest warship in the world. She mounted 136 guns, almost twice the fire-power of his own – by comparison – diminutive two-decker, 74. There were other Spanish three-deckers all more powerful than his own, in close proximity, too, toweringly visible through the smoke and muzzle flash of battle. Whatever might by the consequences for his own flagship, this sudden 'swerve' across the Spanish van forced the mighty *Santissima Trinidad* and the other Spanish ships about her to alter course, giving time for Jervis and the others to catch up and join the fight which now rapidly developed. The *Culloden*, first in line, was already closely engaged, Troubridge's gunners hurling rapid broadsides at the *San Nicolas*, 80.

Nelson sorely needed this support. If the Spanish ships had been

ABOVE Nelson's ship, the *Captain* (on the left), falls upon the *San Josef* and the *San Nicolas* before boarding them in turn.
LEFT The *Victory* raking the larger Spanish ship *Salvador del Mundo* during the hotly contested battle.

RIGHT *The Dying Sailor*, a watercolour, *c.* 1790, by Thomas Rowlandson who had visited many naval bases and saw at first hand the rough conditions endured by sailors.

as well manned, and led by as able and determined officers as the British ships, the *Captain* would soon have been dismasted and smashed beyond recovery. But now, in turn, she passed across the bows of the *San Josef*, 112, the *Salvador del Mundo*, 112 and the *San Nicolas* to engage the *Santissima Trinidad*, towering above her like a frigate beside a cutter.

This mêlée, this close fighting – 'you could not put a bodkin between us', 'a man might jump from one ship to the other' as Collingwood described two close brushes – was relished by the British and feared by the Spaniards. Collingwood described how his shot once passed through two Spanish ships, so close were they packed, causing fearful carnage. 'Our fire carried all before it,' he wrote of his point-blank engagement with the *San Ysidro*, 74, 'and in ten minutes she hauled down her colours.'

This same well-regulated and rapid fire forced the *San Josef* and *San Nicolas* to fall on one another, locked together. Nelson at once seized the opportunity this offered. 'At this time,' he later told the Duke of Clarence, 'the *Captain*, having lost her foretop mast, not a

sail, shroud or rope left, her wheel shot away, and incapable of further service in the line, or in chase, I ordered Captain Miller to put the helm hard a-starboard, and, calling for boarders, ordered them to board.'

Drawing his sword, Nelson himself was among the first to jump into the enemy's mizzen chains with Edward Berry ('an officer of talents, great courage and laudable ambition', Nelson had reported of him). A soldier had broken the upper quarter gallery window of the Spaniard, and Nelson followed him through it, smashing open the locked doors within. The Spanish officers fired their pistols as they retreated before this terrifying onslaught.

'Having pushed on to the quarterdeck,' ran Nelson's report, 'I found Captain Berry in possession of the poop, and the Spanish ensign hauling down. I passed on to the larboard gangway to the forecastle, where I met two or three Spanish officer prisoners to my seamen, and they delivered me their swords.' Thus wrote Nelson, his matter-of-fact report concealing the tumult and fury of this hand-to-hand struggle.

An engraving of Nelson's distinguished action when capturing the *San Nicolas* at the Battle of Cape St Vincent.

With the *San Nicolas* in his hands, musket and pistol fire was opened from the *San Josef* still locked to her side. It came mainly from the stern gallery, and Nelson at once ordered this second great ship to be boarded in turn. He led the way himself – 'Westminster Abbey or Glorious Victory!', his favourite cry in hand-to-hand combat – Berry helping him again into the main chains. The fight was short and fierce.

A Spanish officer looked over from the quarterdeck rail and said they surrendered. From this most welcome intelligence it was not long before I was on the quarterdeck, where the Spanish Captain, with a bow, presented me with his sword, and said the Admiral was dying of his wounds below. I asked him on his honour if the ship were surrendered? He declared she was, on which I gave him my hand and desired him to call his officers and ship's company to tell them of it, which he did; and on the quarterdeck of a Spanish first-rate, extravagant as the story may seem, did I receive the swords of vanquished Spaniards; which, as I received, I gave to William Fearney, one of my bargemen, who put them with the greatest sangfroid under his arm.

Two more Spanish ships of the line were seized as prizes with others breaking free from the mêlée. For a time, later in the afternoon, the battle centred about the *Santissima Trinidad*. The intrepid Captain James Saumarez caused her to strike her colours but to his chagrin she rehoisted her own flag when he was called away by Jervis. The second, easterly division, was now belatedly showing signs of fight, or at least of saving their greatest vessel, which they succeeded in towing away from the battle area.

It was now late in the afternoon. Darkness would soon fall, and the seas were still high. Although British casualties had been amazingly small – a mere seventy-three dead – the men were weary and stunned by the noise and fury of battle, many of their ships crippled, with sails torn to tatters, and fallen masts and spars cluttering the decks. A pursuit of sound Spanish ships under these conditions was likely to be profitless, and Jervis ordered the fleet to withdraw with its prizes.

As the flagship passed the battered *Captain*, the men of the *Victory* gave the two-decker three cheers for its heroic capture of two of the enemy more powerful than itself.

'At dusk', Nelson later reported with satisfaction, 'I went on board the *Victory*, when the Admiral received me on the quarterdeck, and having embraced me, said he could not sufficiently thank

OVERLEAF Nelson receiving the sword of surrender from the Spanish captain on the quarterdeck of the captured *San Josef* after he had led a successful boarding party onto the ship.

me, and used every kind expression which could not fail to make me happy.' The breaking of the rules had been justified in the event, and Jervis was right to be magnanimous. Signals and instructions were made to be broken when a commander clearly saw that this was the right thing to do. But only great commanders had the courage to do so.

Nelson's use of one enemy first-rate to seize another soon found waggish definition in the Fleet, and throughout Britain. It was 'Nelson's Patent Bridge for boarding first-rates'. 'Too flattering', was Nelson's own comment. But how he loved it!

With the Spanish Fleet battered and demoralized and unable to join with the French and Dutch for the invasion, Sir John Jervis was created an earl, and took as his title St Vincent for the cape off which the battle had been fought. Nelson was created a Knight of the Bath for his part in the action, and was confirmed in his flag rank of rear-admiral. St Valentine and St Vincent had together brought Nelson fame. For the five years and eight months left to him his legend was to grow greater with every victory.

His father, wintering in the West Country, wrote of 'the height of glory to which your professional judgment, united with a proper degree of bravery, guarded by Providence, few sons, my dear child, attain to, and fewer fathers live to see . . .'

Little more than 200 miles off the coast of Africa is the small volcanic island of Tenerife, one of the Canary Islands, notable to

The island of Tenerife and its distinctive mountain, the Pico de Teide.

mariners for its 12,000-foot snow-clad Pico de Teide, so often the first point of identification for ships returning to Europe from the Cape, and for its magnificent harbour of Santa Cruz. It had for long been a prized possession of the Spanish Empire, and a staging post for the traffic to Spain's rich possessions in South and Central America.

After the Battle of Cape St Vincent, the British Fleet was chiefly occupied in blockading the Spanish Fleet in Cadiz. It was in the course of this blockade that Nelson further enhanced his reputation with his personal seizure of the Spanish gunboat. In April 1797 Nelson and Jervis conceived a stratagem to damage further the Spanish cause. It was a plan with overtones of Drake and Hawkins, Frobisher and (more recently) Anson, to storm Santa Cruz and seize or destroy the port's shipping, and especially the homeward-bound Manila treasure ship. Anson had captured this ship on its Pacific leg from the Philippines (the Manila treasure was of course carted by land across Panama) and had become one of the richest men in England as a consequence.

The plan was for Nelson to sail with seven ships of the line and frigates, with a strong company of marines and sailors for the shore attack. There was a fort guarding the entrance to the harbour, and it was intended first to put boats ashore and storm this in a surprise attack at night.

On the night of 21 July 1797 it was pitch dark, and the expedition had approached unnoticed to within a mile of the proposed landing place for the attack on the fort. Nelson's ultimatum to the Governor of the island, demanding the immediate surrender of the Manila treasure ship *El Principe d'Asturias* had been rejected: 'The horrors of war, which will fall on the inhabitants . . . for I shall destroy Santa Cruz, and the other towns in the island, by a bombardment...'

But meanwhile a gale had got up and, with an adverse current, prohibited the landing ships from getting any closer to the shore. They persisted in their attempt until daylight, when any remaining element of surprise was lost, and the ships temporarily withdrew. But Nelson, his confidence and determination undiminished, pressed on with the attack in daylight, in spite of the fact that he could not get his big ships close enough to support the shore party with a bombardment.

The attackers suffered casualties and made no progress, and Nelson was forced to withdraw them. He would lead the attack. He would lead an attack, at night this time, on the harbour mole, and thence to the town itself.

He dined on board the *Seahorse* in the highest spirits with his old friend Fremantle, two men who had so often and so successfully fought together. Fremantle had his wife Betsey with him, a spirited, volatile woman, a favourite with all the Fleet. 'The Admiral supped with us,' she wrote, 'he then went with Fremantle on their expedition. They are all to land in the Town. As the taking of this place seemed an easy and almost sure thing, I went to bed after they were gone, apprehending no danger for Fremantle.'

A sure thing? The officers must have been more reassuring than the situation warranted. No more than an hour later, both men had been wounded in the arm. Some of the men of the attacking parties had survived to storm the mole and spike the guns. Many more had died in the fierce fire of the well-prepared Spanish positions. A cutter sank with most of its crew and landing party. No one could live for long in this fierce fusillade. Nelson was stepping out of his boat, sword drawn, when he was struck by a piece of grapeshot. It penetrated a little above the elbow, severing an artery and compound-fracturing the bone.

The admiral fell back into the bottom of the boat, bleeding freely. 'I am a dead man!' he cried. Young Josiah was at his side. He had come on the attack against Nelson's wishes, and now was to prove his saviour. Acting with great speed and enterprise, he used his silk scarf to make a tourniquet. One of the bargemen extemporized a sling, and they made Nelson as comfortable as possible, with the shot and shell still filling the air and killing and wounding many of those about them.

The boat was launched. The men bent to their oars. 'To the *Seahorse*!' Josiah ordered. But as they approached the ship in the darkness, Nelson cried out that he must not go on board this ship, not without news for Mrs Fremantle of her husband, and himself in this condition.

'You will risk your life if we go farther.'

'Then I will die, for I would rather suffer death than alarm Mrs Fremantle.'

Later, they tried to help him up the gangway of the *Theseus*. Nelson shouldered them aside. 'I have yet my legs left, and one arm. Tell the surgeon to make haste and get his instruments. I know I must lose my right arm, so the sooner it is off the better.'

Giant rummer glass engraved with the scene of Nelson being wounded at Tenerife on 24 July 1797.

On the quarterdeck he returned the salutes with his left arm for the first time. In the red-painted cockpit, the surgeon laid out his instruments, and the Admiral was held while with knife and saw the surgeon took off the arm between elbow and shoulder. Nelson withstood the pain with predictable stoicism. The worst part was the coldness of the instruments, and later he gave instructions that surgeons must always warm their instruments before amputations. Alas! there was rarely time for this luxury in combat.

The attack had been a catastrophe. Of the 650 or so men who had embarked, only half eventually fought their way to the Great

Square of Santa Cruz. Here they had re-formed for an attack upon the Citadel 'but found it far beyond their power to take'.

The Spanish Governor, meanwhile, had been more than forbearing. He was almost extravagantly courteous, allowing the British to withdraw when they recognized the hopelessness of their situation, and even giving them boats to replace those that had been smashed in the surf in the disembarkation.

At first recovering well from his operation, Nelson wrote a message with his left hand to the Governor:

> Sir,
> I cannot take my departure from this Island, without returning your Excellency my sincerest thanks for your attention towards me, by your humanity in favour of our wounded men in your power, or under your care, and for your generosity towards all our people who were disembarked, which I shall not fail to represent to my Sovereign, hoping also, at a proper time, to assure your Excellency in person how truly I am, Sir, your most obedient, humble servant,
>
> Horatio Nelson
> P.S. I trust your Excellency will do me the honour to accept a Cask of English beer and cheese.

Formally, Nelson told Jervis of the sad fact of failure. 'I am under the painful necessity of acquainting you that we have not been able to succeed in our attack.' Informally, emotionally, on the same day (27 July 1797), he wrote to his Commander-in-Chief, 'I am become a burthen to my friends, and useless to my Country . . . When I leave your command, I become dead to the World; I go hence and am no more seen . . . I hope you will be able to give me a frigate, to convey the remains of my carcase to England.' Then there is an apology for his left-handed 'scrawl'.

Fremantle's wound was not severe, but Jervis decided that both officers should return to England, so together with the ever-solicitous Betsey (heavy with child) they embarked in the *Seahorse*. Nelson fretted at the contrary winds, and the pain from his wound made him short-tempered. The fact was that the stump was not healing as it should. One of the ligatures could not be removed, a

After losing his right arm, Nelson managed to eat using this gold combined knife and fork sent to him by an admirer.

A drawing of Nelson in 1797 by Grignon.

certain amount of poisoning had set in, and he needed opiates to sleep at night.

But the sight of English shores cheered him. The *Seahorse* anchored at Spithead on 1 September 1797 and, after dinner, Nelson was rowed ashore, to step onto English soil for the first time for more than four years. With his personal servant, Seaman Tom Allen, he took the stage to Bath, where Fanny and his father were both staying, and arrived on the evening of the 3rd.

4

The Hero of the Nile

29 March 1798 was a day of dark skies and driving rain. Rear-Admiral Sir Horatio Nelson KCB hoisted his blue flag in the ship of the line HMS *Vanguard* at Spithead. His country's dangers remained as great as ever. It was known that Napoleon Bonaparte had just visited the Channel ports to study again the possibility of invasion. Once ashore on this island, what was there to prevent the Grand Army, which had triumphed wherever it had marched, from grasping the greatest prize of all – the kingdom of Great Britain and all its priceless colonies? To the south, the Mediterranean remained a French sea, the Royal Navy without a base there.

'I am very happy to send you Sir Horatio Nelson,' the First Lord communicated to Jervis, Lord St Vincent.

St Vincent, still commanding the forces responsible for watching the Spanish fleet in Cadiz, later signalled, 'The arrival of Admiral Nelson has given me new life.'

After the healing of his stump, Nelson did not have to wait long or agitate for a new command. Not this time. In December 1797 he had been given the *Vanguard* as his flagship, and on the 17th, while in London from Bath, he had inspected her at Chatham. Two days later he was at St Paul's Cathedral in company with King George III returning thanks for his country's great naval victories. During the following weeks the ship was worked up for foreign service. Among the preparations was Nelson's own characteristic request: to the Society for the Propagation of Christian Knowledge for as many Bibles and Prayer Books as could be spared for the men under his command.

While Nelson was sailing down Channel and across the Bay of Biscay with a convoy during the second half of April, Bonaparte's intentions became known through Britain's spy network in Europe. The proposed invasion of England had been postponed. A great

ABOVE A French watch inscribed 'Descente en Angle-terre', anticipating the French invasion of England.
FACING PAGE A romanticized painting of the wounded Nelson after the Battle of the Nile.

72

number of transports had been collected in Toulon and Genoa, and some 30,000 troops were to be embarked and to sail under cover of the French fleet. The destination? None of the reports was definite. But the force must be intercepted at sea, and destroyed. The Mediterranean must be re-entered by a powerful force, in spite of the absence of a base. Jervis received a directive from the Admiralty:

> Your lordship is to lose no time in detaching from your Fleet a Squadron, consisting of 12 Sail-of-the-line, and a competent number of Frigates, under the command of some discreet Flag-Officer, into the Mediterranean, with instructions to him to proceed in quest of the said Armament; and on falling in with it . . . to take or destroy it . . .

All this was known throughout the fleet when Nelson joined St Vincent's fleet off Cadiz. But the choice of the commander of this fleet had yet to be made. Almost all the admirals were senior to Nelson. Several of them were piqued when it became known that the admiral who had shared the Commander-in-Chief's victory off Cape St Vincent the previous summer had been appointed 'the discreet Flag-Officer', the commander of this powerful detachment with its exciting and exacting task.

At first the fates seemed to be against him, and within twelve days of departure catastrophe struck. He had only just arrived on his blockading station off Toulon when his frigates brought him the news that the French fleet was still there. A captured officer confirmed the size of the armada – no fewer than three hundred transports – and this news was followed by an overnight gale.

Let Nelson himself describe the events in a letter to Fanny, in a style and manner that tells much of the man:

> Vanguard, Island of St Peter's, in Sardinia,
> May 24, 1798

> My dearest Fanny,
> I ought not to call what has happened to the Vanguard by the cold name of accident: I believe firmly, that it was the Almighty's goodness, to check my consummate vanity. I hope it has made me a better Officer, as I feel confident it has made me a better Man. I kiss with all humility the rod.
> Figure to yourself a vain man, on Sunday evening at sun-set, walking in his cabin with a Squadron about him, who looked up to their Chief to lead them to glory, and in whom this Chief placed the firmest reliance, that the proudest Ships, in equal numbers, belonging to France, would

have bowed to their flags; and with a very rich Prize lying by him. Figure to yourself this proud, conceited man, when the sun rose on Monday morning, his Ship dismasted, his Fleet dispersed, and himself in such distress, that the meanest Frigate out of France would have been a very unwelcome guest . . .

    With kind love to my Father, believe me

ever your affectionate husband
Horatio Nelson

But he was also able to reassure Fanny that, by dint of the greatest efforts of his men, and especially of two of his captains, Sir James Saumarez and John Ball, who had towed the flagship out of its worst dangers, he hoped to be at sea again within two days.

The god of misfortune remained unplacated. This, in stark facts, is the sequence of frustration and dismay that followed over the next weeks:

His frigates, concluding from his condition that he would return to Gibraltar, proceeded there themselves, depriving the squadron of its eyes – its scouting force.

The gale that had dismasted the *Vanguard* proved a blessing for the French, and Bonaparte, with his naval Commander Admiral François Brueys d'Aigaïlliers, broke through the scattered and unsighted blockading Squadron.

This calamity was in no way eased by Nelson's continuing lack of intelligence about the enemy's destination. Sicily? Malta? Egypt? By way of the Dardanelles to Russia? By way of the Strait of Gibraltar to the West Indies?

Without frigates, he had to send a ship of the line to discover the situation at Malta. The island had fallen to the French, who had installed a garrison and left – for where?

An engraving by Nodet showing Bonaparte capturing Malta from the Knights of St John on 19 June 1798.

Nelson, calculating that Alexandria was the armada's destination, sailed east at great speed, confident that Bonaparte's designs were on Egypt, and then on establishing military control of India.

He was right. At night, in dirty weather, his squadron passed so close to the French armada that the enemy heard the British signal guns firing in order to maintain station. The French remained silent.

He was off Alexandria by 28 June 1798. The harbour was empty. Letters to the First Lord, to St Vincent, to Sir William Hamilton at Naples, all reflect his puzzlement and anger. 'My hopes of information were vain'; 'I have heard by a Vessel just spoke with, that the French Fleet were seen off the north End of Sicily'; 'The last account I had of the French Fleet, was from a Tunisian Cruizer'; 'I have reason to believe, from not seeing a Vessel, that they have heard of my coming up the Mediterranean, and are got safe into Corfu' – the last of these with the additional *cri de coeur* to the Consul at Alexandria, 'But still I am most exceedingly anxious to know from you if any reports or preparations have been made on Egypt for them.'

Throughout July, Nelson's squadron, now augmented by more 74s, and commanded by the cream of St Vincent's captains and

A painting by Giacomo Guardi showing the British Fleet led by Rear-Admiral Sir Horatio Nelson KB, as he now was, at anchor in the Bay of Naples on 17 June 1798 awaiting news of the whereabouts of the French fleet; Vesuvius can be seen in the background.

Nelson's Band of Brothers, pursued the French will-o'-the-wisp the length and breadth of the eastern Mediterranean. Whatever qualities the French might lack as seamen and fighters, their elusiveness was uncanny. How could such a vast armada seemingly be lost to the world for so long? That is what people were now asking.

At home, as dispatches arrived confirming that the Toulon fleet was still undetected and at large, an anxious, almost acid, note crept into public comment. 'It is a remarkable circumstance', ran one article, 'that a fleet of near 400 sail, covering a space of so many leagues, should have been able to elude the knowledge of our fleet for such a long space of time.'

But Nelson's resolve and optimism never diminished. After the third week of failure, he was still able to write to Sir William and Emma Hamilton at Naples:

> My dear Friends,
> Thanks to your exertions, we have victualled and watered: and surely watering at the Fountain of Arethusa [Syracuse], we must have victory. We shall sail with the first breeze, and be assured I will return either crowned with laurel, or covered with cypress . . .

A week later, Nelson experienced the first break in his long sequence of misfortune. Off the Greek coast, he sent a ship into the Gulf of Koroni, where a small French prize was taken. It was full of wine, and something even more welcome: news that, some four weeks earlier, Bonaparte's armada was seen sailing south-east from Crete. Its destination could only be Egypt. Some 350 vessels and more than 50,000 Frenchmen had escaped through the net, the troops would now long since have been landed, long since have conquered Egypt. But what of the armada?

Nelson had been right, but he had been too quick, and his failure could be ascribed to the loss of his frigates – and to the Almighty's constant concern for his humility?

Noon, 1 August 1798. A blazing hot day. Twenty-five ships of the line, fine-honed by the greatest naval commander in the world into a shiningly brilliant fighting force, raised the Egyptian coast. There was that towering monument again, the Pharos of Alexandria. The harbour was empty of the French fleet, as it had been before, but this time there was no cause for disappointment.

Exactly two and a half hours later, the foremost ship made a signal. Yes, said the fluttering flags, the French are here. Here in strength. They were anchored in Aboukir Bay.

Edward Berry, Nelson's flag-captain, noted: 'The utmost joy seemed to animate every breast on board the squadron at sight of the Enemy, and the pleasure which the Admiral himself felt was perhaps the more heightened than that of any other man.'

There was to be no hesitation, no delay, no overture, no formal manoeuvring in the traditional manner of eighteenth-century sea warfare. His squadron would sail straight into battle, with time enough to clear for action, run out the guns, sand the decks (blood being so slippery), to stow the hammocks about the upper decks as protection against splinters, to hoist out the boats and tow them astern. It would be what Admiral Brueys must least expect, and for that reason alone would give them an added advantage.

And how confident was Admiral Brueys in his tactical situation? We shall never know. Bonaparte, years later and *en route* to his confinement on St Helena, claimed that his admiral calculated that to be caught at anchor in Aboukir Bay would prove fatal. It is equally likely that, in his final defeat, Bonaparte found it comforting to ascribe the blame to others.

By any reckoning, the position of the French fleet, if not impregnable, was highly advantageous. Aboukir Bay is like an open mouth pointing to the east. The upper lip is shoal, broken by a small island, and shoal fills much of the inner bay. The French fleet of thirteen ships was anchored in a single line almost at the entrance to the bay, protected by these shoals on two sides, by numerous gunboats and frigates and a formidable battery of guns and mortars.

There was little to choose in numbers between the two fleets, but Nelson's ships were, on average, smaller, and in weight of broadside considerably less. In the centre of the line, flying the French admiral's flag, was the mighty *L'Orient* of 120 guns, almost as large and quite as powerful as the *Santissima Trinidad*. The British had nothing to equal it.

Brueys was more than taken aback by Nelson's impetuosity at sailing straight into battle; he seemed to be stunned into inactivity. It appeared that he intended to fight as a static force, as if his fleet were a wooden fortress. There were French watering parties still ashore, but the men would not, by his reckoning, be missed as only the outward facing guns would need to be in action.

There was a light breeze – 'a top-gallant breeze' – from directly

An engraving of Admiral François Brueys, Commander of the French fleet during the Egypt expedition.

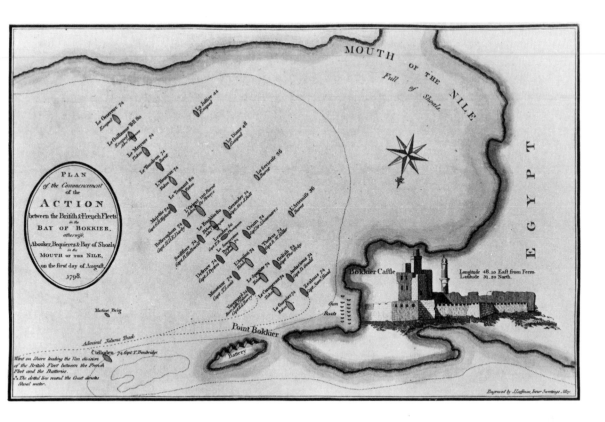

A contemporary map published in October 1798 showing the position of the British and French fleets in Aboukir Bay.

OVERLEAF *The Battle of the Nile*, painted by Nicholas Pocock; Captain Foley surprised the anchored French fleet by sailing the *Goliath* round to attack from the leeward side.

astern of Nelson's fleet as it sailed slowly, majestically, in a single line towards the massed masts and yards of the French. There was little for the men to do but sit by their guns, stripped to the waist in the heat, and watch through the gunports as the French vessels slowly grew bigger. For many this was to be their first action, for others the last. Those who had fought in fleet actions before were now full of anecdotes, some of them bearing upon French vessels they were facing for a second or third time. There was ready ammunition, shot racks uncovered, guns run out and free of the tampions in their muzzles: 12-pounders and 24-pounders, the 36-pounders on the lowest decks, the mighty carronades. But powder in silk bags for only two or three broadsides because of the risk of explosion, the little agile 'powder monkeys', as young as twelve years old, standing by ready to dash down to the magazines.

The men in the chains had no time for chat and speculation. They were busy sounding every few minutes, for these waters were little known and notoriously dangerous and changeable. Since the *Vanguard* had hauled the wind, taking in her royals to do so, there had

79

been little to do aloft. Now, as they approached more closely to the French line, the men went aloft preparatory to taking in sail, and others stood by to get out a bower cable and bend it forward, for Nelson intended to anchor close alongside the stationary French ships.

But this was to be no slogging match, ship against ship. Nelson's plans were more subtle than that. To ensure victory, he would start on the enemy's van and centre, two ships against one, and smash them to pieces in turn and at leisure. Meanwhile, he was to cause Brueys further shock and dismay. His flag-captain later described

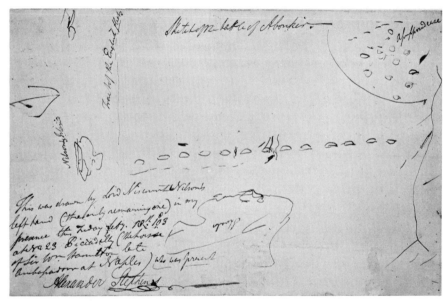

Nelson's own sketch of the start of the Battle of the Nile, drawn with his left hand on his return to England.

the move that was to ensure disaster for the French. 'It instantly struck his eager and penetrating mind, *that where there was room for the enemy's ship to swing, there was room for one of ours to anchor.*' He was, in short, going to risk his ships running aground by sending in some of them on the *inside*, between the shoal and the French line, correctly judging that no provision would have been made for fighting the port guns.

The degree of risk was established before the first shot had been fired when Troubridge's *Culloden* went aground on the shoal at the entrance to the bay. In spite of the most strenuous efforts of this gallant captain and his officers and men to refloat this man-of-war, she remained incapable of taking any part in the battle. Meanwhile, soon after half past five, with sunset less than an hour away, Nelson signalled for close action. When darkness closed about them, four identification lights would be hoisted on each ship.

Foley's *Goliath* was first in the van. There was no more experienced captain than Tom Foley, no one who better understood and appreciated Nelson's thinking. How he relished the shock the French would receive when he took his ship inshore of *Le Guerrier*! But there was to be unpleasantness before that satisfaction, for his ship, and others in the van – the *Zealous* and *Theseus*, the *Orion* and *Audacious* – must pay the inevitable price of this bold approach, and 'receive into their bows the whole fire of the broadsides of the French line'.

These French gunners were unlike the Spaniards at the Battle of Cape St Vincent. These were Bonaparte's gunners, the best-trained in the French Navy, and the British who had been in both engagements were quick to recognize the uncomfortable contrast.

The great red sun was just touching the western horizon when the *Goliath* headed straight for *Le Guerrier*'s anchor cable, and almost at once fired a full ripple broadside. These were some of the fastest gunners in the world. The moment the cannon, with a deafening crash, was pulled up in its massive recoil by the cables, the crew were at work, cleaning and dampening down the muzzle, and at once driving home, in turn, the silk cartridge bags, then the solid shot, and in one cooperative, much-rehearsed movement, running the gun out again, 'clattering of ropes, and grumbling of blocks', three men at the crowbar adjusting the aim, re-securing the cables, preparing the flint match.

Seven o'clock. Darkness had fallen over Egypt, a soft night. But here, on this sandy, featureless stretch of coast the darkness was split apart as if all the ancient Pharaohs were celebrating a great orgy of combat. The continuous ripple of muzzle flash, the steadier flame of fires, together lighting the base of the rising cloud of smoke, stemmed from this ferocious combat between some 20,000 Frenchmen and Englishmen a thousand miles from their homes, few of whom knew or cared anything for Egypt.

A thousand Frenchmen were probably already dead or mortally wounded. They were fighting for their lives and their ships with fanatical ardour, and everywhere in the French ships there were examples of supreme gallantry and self-sacrifice.

The commanders were, as always, the most vulnerable, and gave

heroic examples to their men. Captain Dupetit Thouars of *Le Tonnant* was hit again and again until he had only one limb not shattered. But he would not allow himself to be taken below, instead ordering a tub of bran in which he had himself placed and then continued to direct the battle from it. He bled slowly to death, his last order: 'Nail the colours to the mast – no surrender!' Among the British to suffer was Captain Westcott of the *Majestic*, who fell with a musket ball in his throat.

The two Commanders-in-Chief were both struck at about the same time in the evening. Nelson, with Berry at his side, was hit on the head by a fragment of flying langrage, a shot used by privateers, and by the French, to tear sail. It cut him deep to the scalp above his old wound, the pouring blood blinding his good eye.

The fighting went on into the night as seen in this painting by Henry Whitcomb, showing the end of the action and the victorious British ships in the foreground.

Berry caught him before he fell, and heard his admiral murmur, 'I am killed. Remember me to my wife.' He was carried down to the cockpit, where some forty of his men lay groaning, awaiting or recovering from the knife, or simply dying. The air was thick with the smell of blood, of expended powder charge, lantern smoke and, as always, the press of male bodies.

'Do not identify me to the Surgeons,' he told Berry. 'I will await my turn.'

On board the mighty *L'Orient*, the French Commander-in-Chief was suffering more gravely. He, too, was wounded in the head, and then twice more in the body. And he, too, believed that he was dying. Like Thouars, he would not allow himself to be taken below, and merely ordered an arms chest to sit upon in order to continue to direct the battle.

L'Orient, like a tethered bull set upon by terriers, was receiving in turn the fire of the *Bellerophon, Swiftsure, Alexander* and *Leander*. Her suffering was awful to witness. Ball and grape shot were tearing the monster to pieces, musket fire was decimating any who exposed themselves on the flagship's deck. A cannon ball struck Brueys, his fourth and this time fatal injury, for it cut him almost in two. Already, his flagship was on fire, and he died with the bitter knowledge of inevitable defeat.

At around half past eight, with the contest at its height and the sound and fury of battle ceaseless, Surgeon Jefferson began to probe Nelson's wound. A large flap of flesh had fallen over his good eye, adding further conviction to Nelson's belief that he was as good as

An engraving of the wounded captain of *Le Tonnant*; mortally wounded, and having already lost a leg, he made his men promise never to surrender to the English and to throw his body into the sea.

dead. Jefferson sewed it back into place and cleaned the wound. It was not even a dangerous wound, he was assured, let alone a fatal one.

Still Nelson was certain that he was nearing his end, and called for the chaplain to take his last messages. The chaplain came with company. The sound of cheers was rising above the thunder of cannon. Berry was at Nelson's side again, with what he called 'pleasing intelligence'. He had sent a boarding party onto *Le Spartiate*, and an officer had returned with the French captain's sword, which Berry now presented to his admiral. Two more French ships had been taken for sure, and *L'Orient*, *Le Tonnant* and *L'Heureux* 'are considered completely in our power . . . It appears, Sir, that victory has already declared itself in our favour.'

Now Nelson could die happy, as the hero at the height of victory: the glory, the drama, the fitting timing, were all that he could pray for. The Almighty had indeed been generous to this undeserving servant. The scene now being enacted was the ultimate manifestation of his boyhood dream on board the *Dolphin*.

During the evening of the battle Nelson was badly wounded in the head; he is seen here awaiting medical treatment in the cockpit.

86

An engraving by
Daniel Orme showing
Nelson returning to
the quarter-deck of his
ship, the *Vanguard*, to
witness the final
moments of the French
flagship, *L'Orient*,
before she blew up.

The surgeon insisted on his removal to a quieter place, to recover
further from the shock and concussion. From the *Vanguard*'s bread
room, Admiral Nelson summoned his secretary. The man came, but
the sight of this frail, pale figure, a great bandage across his head,
and evidently in the last extremity, was too much for him. He was
summarily sacked later: 'He has not activity for me . . .' And we can
hear Nelson snort.

Instead, Nelson himself seized a pen, and in his own hand began
to write his dispatch to St Vincent: 'My Lord, Almighty God has
blessed His Majesty's Arms in the late battle . . .'

Above, the battle raged on in the night. Not a British sailor could
know that their commander was already pronouncing victory with
his shaky left hand on parchment. He had scarcely begun when
Berry reappeared once again. 'The enemy flagship is on fire, Sir . . .'

This was too great a sight to miss. 'I must be assisted on deck . . .'
He required little assistance.

It was now a quarter past nine and the fire, starting in the after
part of *L'Orient*'s cabin, was rapidly devouring the after part of the

OVERLEAF 'The sea
became an illuminated
wasteland of broken
masts and spars and
timbers, cables and
burnt rigging, black
shrivelled corpses and
struggling figures.'

87

ship. There could be no greater satisfaction for a commander-in-chief than to observe the end of his opponent's flagship – 'completely beat' as he put it. But there were compassionate considerations, too. Urgent ones, for the French crew were already plunging into the brightly lit water about the conflagration. Berry was ordered 'to make every possible exertion' to 'save as many as possible'.

Berry did what he could, but the battle still raged, and some indefatigable crews were gallantly working the guns on the monster's lower deck. In the one serviceable boat Berry's men succeeded in picking up some seventy Frenchmen, some swimming, some clutching debris, while the flames swept the length of L'Orient, racing like yellow snakes up the rigging, gripping the topmasts. Figures, in ever-increasing numbers, were seen leaping into the sea, all gunfire now ceased; and on the quarterdeck the flag-captain, Louis de Casabiance, and his ten-year-old son Jacques, were creating the legend that many years later led Felicia Dorothea Hemans to compose a heroic poem:

> The boy stood on the burning deck
> Whence all but he had fled . . .

The final detonation was as inevitable as it was awesome. Ten miles away French soldiers were startled and mystified by the sound. In at least one British ship, men below decks thought their own magazine had gone up. Though half-blinded by the flash, those who witnessed the explosion spoke of burning debris and bodies being hurled high into the air. The sea became an illuminated wasteland of broken masts and spars and timbers, cables and burned rigging, black shrivelled corpses and struggling figures. The smell of smoke and death hung heavy in the still night air.

L'Orient had been painting ship when Nelson arrived at Aboukir Bay, and the fire had spread to open buckets, and finally to the ship's magazine. She had on board the loot Bonaparte had pillaged on his campaigns: £600,000 in gold and diamonds alone. The loss of this treasure, intended to finance Bonaparte's newest adventure, compounded the loss of the flagship and her Admiral.

'After this awful scene,' Berry wrote, 'the firing was recommenced with the ships to leeward of the Centre, till twenty past ten, when there was a total cessation of firing for about ten minutes: after which it was revived till about three in the morning.'

The cause of these lulls was simple. The men fighting on both

sides, as if by silent treaty, ceased firing from sheer exhaustion. They fell round their guns, and amid the litter and blood of combat, slept, the battle still unconcluded.

But by three o'clock in the morning several more French ships had struck their colours, and others had been overwhelmed. Nelson, certain now of the greatest victory since the repulse of the Spanish Armada, remained on deck until this time, when he was persuaded to go below to rest. He left a scene of utter desolation, illuminated now by the moon, in which several of his own ships appeared in worse shape than some of the enemy's. The *Bellerophon* could do no more. Even before *L'Orient* blew up, she had lost all her

A patch box commemorating the victory of the Battle of the Nile.

masts and cables, and had drifted to the lee side of the bay. When the French ships of the line *Le Généreux* and *Guillaume Tell* and two frigates cut their cables and left the line, only the *Zealous* was in a state to pursue them, and she had to be recalled.

'My people were so extremely jaded', wrote one British captain, 'that as soon as they had hove our sheet anchor up, they dropped under the capstan-bars and were asleep in a moment, in every sort of posture, having been working then at their fullest exertion, or fighting, for near 12 hours.'

Both sides, then, had fought the other to a standstill. But the statistics taken at dawn were undeniable. Nine French big ships captured, two burned, two escaped. Two out of four frigates burned or captured. French losses were 5,225 men, mostly drowned or burned to death, almost half of those engaged. (One British captain described the state of his prize, 'The slaughter on board her is *dreadful*; her Captain is dying.')

British dead were 200 and 700 or so wounded, out of 5,000 present, excluding Nelson who would not now allow his name to be included among the casualties. A captain visiting him in his cot described him as 'weak but in good spirits'. There was good reason for both conditions.

Those who recorded the scene off Aboukir Bay after the battle told of the utter weariness on both sides, of the slow, effortful retrieval of bodies from the litter-strewn water and the sandy shores, of the patching of torn sails, the clearing of decks and replacement of smashed masts and spars with spares, the organizing of prize crews for the captured French ships. It was slow going on the first day after the night-long battle, and continued throughout 3 and 4 August.

Nelson emerged from his cabin early on the morning of the 2nd, his face drawn and pale beneath the head bandage, acknowledging the cheers given by his men wherever he went. There was more to do after a battle won than a battle lost: a truce to be established with the commandants at Aboukir and Alexandria to enable the wounded to be sent ashore with their own surgeons for proper care, reports on the condition of his ships to be studied, his captains to be received, their congratulations to be gracefully accepted and the niceties of the replies to be prepared. But the first and most important consideration: the Almighty to be thanked.

> At two o'clock accordingly on that day, public service was performed on the quarter-deck of the Vanguard [ran Berry's report] by the Rev. Mr Comyn, the other ships following the example of the Admiral . . . This solemn act of gratitude to Heaven seemed to make a very deep impression upon several of the prisoners, both officers and men, some of the former of whom remarked, 'that it was no wonder we could preserve such order and discipline, when we could impress the minds of our men with such sentiments after a victory so great, and at a moment of such seeming confusion.'

Another event that had a salutary effect on the numerous French prisoners was the lighting of fires of celebration along the shoreline by the Arabs as soon as it became known that their late conquerors had been defeated: 'their exultation was almost equal to our own,' reported one British officer.

Vanguard, off the Mouth of the Nile,
2nd day of August, 1798

TO THE CAPTAINS OF THE SHIPS OF THE SQUADRON

The Admiral most heartily congratulates the Captains, Officers, Seamen, and Marines of the Squadron he has the honour to command, on the event of the late Action; and he desires they will accept his most sincere and cordial Thanks for their very gallant behaviour in this glorious Battle. It must strike forcibly every British Seaman, how superior their conduct is, when in discipline and good order, to the riotous behaviour of lawless Frenchmen.

The Squadron may be assured the Admiral will not fail, with his Dispatches, to represent their truly meritorious conduct in the strongest terms to the Commander-in-Chief.

HORATIO NELSON

Now! The victory to be related, the victory to be exploited! Bonaparte trapped in Egypt with not a single brig in which to escape! French Revolutionary seapower in the Mediterranean smashed!

First to be informed must be British eastern interests, especially the East India Company, so gravely at risk from Bonaparte's armies, and now safe. A lieutenant with a good command of languages was dispatched at once to the many British settlements east of Suez. (He did his work well and swiftly, and as a consequence Nelson was voted a gift of £10,000.)

News of the triumph for Europe was, luckily, dispatched in two vessels for safety, the comparatively undamaged *Leander*, smallest of the British ships of the line under the command of Berry, and the brig *Mutine* with young Hoste. By a strange chance of fate, and as a sop for the French, the *Leander* fell in with one of the two powerful 74s that had cut their cables and fled from Aboukir Bay. The *Leander* fought like a tiger, Berry was wounded, but she eventually was forced to submit.

The *Mutine* arrived safely at Naples with the duplicate dispatches, and the news spread from this kingdom like a shock wave through Europe. In Naples the Queen, in London Lord Spencer, First Lord of the Admiralty, both fainted. Emma Hamilton collapsed so heavily – she was very overweight – that she still complained of her bruises weeks later. But the pain and shock did not prevent her from having a bandeau prepared, inscribed 'Nelson and Victory'. She immediately set out in an open carriage, a British

officer on each side, to drive about the city's streets; as grand a
town crier as had ever been seen.

'Joy, joy, joy to you, brave, gallant, immortalised Nelson!' wrote
Lady Spencer. '. . . My heart is absolutely bursting with different
sensations of joy, of gratitude, of pride, of every emotion that ever
warmed the bosom of a British woman, on hearing of her country's
glory – and all produced by you, my dear, good friend.'

It was indeed a great victory, and its results were profound. Yet
one discerns an element of hysteria in the wild celebrations that
continued long after the news arrived officially on 2 October 1798.
It stemmed from a measure of national guilt, and of a sudden relief
from long-built-up fear, of a recovery of national pride. No other
person was to match the fear aroused by the figure of Bonaparte
throughout Europe until Kaiser Wilhelm II and Adolf Hitler of the

93

...srpation of the Plagues of Egypt;—Destruction of Revolutionary Crocodiles;—or—The British Hero cleansing ȳ Mouth of ȳ Nile

The Gallant Nellson bringing home two Uncommon fierce French Crocadiles from the Nile as a Present to the Keng.

FACING PAGE ABOVE
A cartoon by James
Gillray of Nelson's
victory over the
French, showing his
destruction of the
revolutionary
crocodiles.
FACING PAGE BELOW
A cartoon showing
Nelson bringing
French crocodiles
home to England as
prisoners.
BELOW Nelson received
many gifts to com-
memorate the battle,
amongst them being
this silver cup.

twentieth century, and nowhere was it more intense than in Britain, one of the few nations not yet under his tutelage.

The guilt originated in the doubts, now proved false, of Nelson's abilities. The long pursuit had set nerves jangling, and criticism of The Hero of The Battle of St Vincent was spreading, when all the time he was on Boney's heels, ready to strike. And when he did – why, it was annihilation! How sadly they had misjudged him!

Besides the £10,000, and a pension of £2,000, material gifts poured in from grateful and relieved monarchs and grandees – a diamond ornament, a gold-hilted scimitar, a sable pelisse, a dress sword, a musket with ivory and silver mountings, 2,000 sequins to be distributed among the wounded – all from Turkey. There were diamond-studded boxes, a miniature likeness from the Tsar of All the Russias.

Hood had told Fanny that she was likely soon to become Vis-countess Alexandria. This was not to be. She had to be content with remaining Lady Nelson, for a barony was all that Nelson received, because, explained the Admiralty lamely, he had commanded only a detached squadron from the main fleet. Was the old prejudice against the flashy, flamboyant public hero still lingering in Admiralty corridors? Emma Hamilton was outraged: 'Hang them, I say! If I was King of England I would make you the most noble puissant DUKE NELSON, MARQUIS NILE, EARL ALEXANDRIA, VISCOUNT PYRAMID, BARON CROCODILE, and PRINCE VICTORY, that posterity might have you in all forms.'

5

'The Fair Lady Hamilton'

The beautiful city of Naples had an irresistible attraction for Nelson. After the rigours of Egypt, he longed for the comforts and graces and colour of the Court, and his vanity was drawn to the sounds and sights of public and private adulation. The city would be *en fête* for him, as only the Neapolitans could celebrate. Imagine the extravagant reception the King and Queen and the noble families would give him! And that elderly, distinguished Ambassador, Sir William Hamilton, and his fascinating wife: her luscious, full figure, her teasing yet comforting ways, her wit and irreverence, her understanding glances!

The Neapolitan images that were raised in Nelson's tired mind in those early days of August after the battle, caused him to make the far-reaching decision that Saumarez must take the squadron and its prizes to the Commander-in-Chief, while he sailed to Naples in the *Vanguard*, ostensibly because the flagship – he could have shifted his flag – was in such sore need of repair.

Saumarez was dispatched 'up the Mediterranean' with his great undermanned fleet of repaired British ships and French prizes; young Hood, the Admiral's cousin, was ordered to blockade Alexandria and 'to endeavour to intercept the French Convoy with provisions, which is expected to arrive there soon'; and the *Vanguard* with a small division of accompanying ships set course for Naples on 19 August.

Physically, Nelson was not a good healer, nor a good patient. His wound troubled him greatly, and he let all know about it. 'My head', he wrote to St Vincent, 'is splitting, splitting, splitting.' He excused the brevity of a letter to Fanny by the state of his head. Like his return from Tenerife, the voyage was a miserable one, slow and stormy. On the day after he wrote to his wife, a squall struck the division. In minutes, the flagship lost her main topmast, foremast

George Romney, the celebrated portrait painter, painted Emma Hamilton many times.

97

FACING PAGE ABOVE
A view of the city of
Naples, showing Sir
William Hamilton's
residence, the Palazzo
Sessa, behind the
church dome on the
extreme left.

FACING PAGE BELOW
The English garden at
Caserta in Naples was
designed by Sir
William Hamilton;
Vesuvius can be seen
in the background.
OVERLEAF *Nelson and
Emma at Posillipo*
painted by Serres in
1798; the damaged
British fleet was
repaired in the ship-
yards at Posillipo.

and jib-boom, and men who had survived the shot and shell of the
Nile were dashed to the deck or lost overboard.

'I detest this voyage to Naples', he wrote to St Vincent on 20 September, and told him how, to compound his troubles, he had been
taken with a fever. For Nelson, wound or fever, it must prove fatal.
'I never expect, my dear Lord, to see your face again'; and he was
resigned to God's will.

Two days later, all was changed from despair to an ecstasy of
joy – fever, cough, head pains forgotten. The *Vanguard* – 'the wreck
of the Vanguard' he called it, in typical hyperbole – was towed into
the Bay of Naples, followed by the *Audacious* and *Minotaur*, on
22 September. The weather was brilliant, the approach slow and
stately. Some eyewitnesses estimated that there were five hundred
pleasure boats waiting to receive the conquering British. Jubilant
citizens lined the harbour, leaned from decorated balconies rising
tier upon tier. Bands – even the opera-house orchestra – played
appropriate celebratory airs like 'Rule Britannia', 'See the Conquering Hero', and of course, over and over, the British National
Anthem.

Fanny was told of that climactic moment when, first the Hamiltons and then the King of Naples, came alongside his flagship:

> Sir William and Lady Hamilton came out to sea, attended by numerous
> Boats with emblems, &c. They, my most respectable friends, had really
> been laid up and seriously ill; first from anxiety, and then from joy ...
> Alongside came my honoured friends: the scene in the boat was terribly
> affecting; up flew her Ladyship, and exclaiming, 'O God, is it possible?'
> she fell into my arm more dead than alive ...

Fanny was regaled with more eulogies about the fair Lady
Hamilton – 'she is one of the very best women in this world; she is
an honour to her sex'. And in Bath, where Fanny had just begun
her winter sojourn with her father-in-law, she received letters from
Lady Hamilton that added further colour to the picture of her
husband's arrival in Naples, and of his life there. 'Lord Nelson is
adored here,' she was told, 'and looked on as the deliverer of this
Country ... I need not tell your Ladyship how happy Sir William
and myself are at having an opportunity of seeing our dear, respectable, brave friend return here, with so much honour to himself, and
glory for his Country. We only wanted you to be completely happy.'

Balls and receptions for the best people. Meetings and soirées
and banquets and dinners. He stayed with the Hamiltons in style.

His room was on the upper floor with a semi-circular window, the prospect of the bay seen in a mirror. The residence reflected the taste, and the taste for luxury, of the Ambassador, with furniture, tapestries, busts and statues, and paintings of inestimable value: including three of his mistress, now his wife, all painted by Romney, of her as a model before she was twenty, fresh from Wales and comparatively innocent; as Bacchante; and (Nelson's own favourite) as Saint Cecilia. Here was celebrated, on the grandest scale of all, Nelson's fortieth birthday, with 1,800 guests. A column had been carved and engraved with the names of Nelson's captains at the Nile. The highlight of the party was its unveiling, by Emma of course.

It was probably at this time that he made Emma Hamilton his mistress.

Five days later, Nelson was writing again to St Vincent, 'opposite Lady Hamilton, therefore you will not be surprised at the glorious jumble of this letter. Were your Lordship in my place, I much doubt if you could write so well; our hearts and our hands must be all in a flutter.'

Then, in a letter of gratitude from St Vincent to Emma Hamilton, thanking her 'for restoring the health of our invaluable friend', there is a hint of an edge at the end: 'Pray, do not let your fascinating Neapolitan dames approach too near him; for he is made of flesh and blood and cannot resist their temptations.'

Nelson was on land again, and once again the edge of fate was sharp enough to damage him, and his cause. The dangers to his reputation occasioned by the Lady Hamilton affair were still distant. His intervention in Neapolitan politics was to be more immediately damaging. Inevitably, in time, the French must attack the Kingdom of Naples and the Two Sicilies. The Queen ('the only man in Naples', Bonaparte called her) was sister to Marie Antoinette, Queen of France and recently guillotined. It was hardly surprising, therefore, that she was possessed of a deep and abiding hatred of Bonaparte. Maria Carolina it was who really ruled Naples, while her amiable husband King Ferdinand IV enjoyed, among other pursuits, being democratic and mixing with the poor and beggars, and hunting.

The Neapolitan army was theoretically a powerful one. But it required leadership, and this the Queen acquired in the person of

FACING PAGE An engraving after a painting by Angelica Kauffman, a leading artist of the day, showing Emma in her favourite guise as the Comic Muse. INSET Cameo cutters of Naples used Emma's profile as a model. BELOW Emma took as her inspiration for her Attitudes classical figures painted on frescoes and vases found at Pompeii, near Naples.

a Bavarian General Baron Karl Mack von Leiberich. At first Mack had impressed Nelson by his powers of leadership. His arrival in Naples coincided with new threats on the independence of the kingdom. Some months earlier, Bonaparte's General Louis Berthier had occupied Rome and deposed the Pope. Except for Naples, the Vatican was the last Italian state to fall to the revolutionary forces.

The King of Naples favoured a pre-emptive strike against the French army. The Queen had hotly favoured it long before. Emma Hamilton, acting the familiar part of political intriguer, reminded the Royal Family that they had the greatest-ever victor over the French in their midst, and worked on Nelson's vanity to persuade him to act as adviser. More buoyant than ever with self-confidence, and half convinced that there must be an element of truth in the praise heaped upon him over the past weeks, Nelson advised – 'March now!'

The Queen loved his forthrightness. The King sought glory in the field. On 23 November 1798 General Mack von Leiberich marched across the frontier in five columns with his powerful force. A little over two weeks later, Ferdinand was marching with Neapolitan pomp into Rome.

At least Nelson was too wise to take part in this land campaign. Instead, he sailed with a strong force to Malta, still in French hands and holding out with little food through a British blockade, now that the Mediterranean was again a British sea. He failed to re-capture the island – that was not to come for two more years – but he received the surrender of the nearby island of Gozo.

By the time Nelson returned to Naples, triumph on land had turned to disaster. Mack had deserted his own army when attacked by a greatly inferior force; the Neapolitans were thrown out of Rome in short measure. Nelson sent Troubridge first rumours of the rout. 'It is reported, and, indeed, is certain, that the Neapolitan Officers, and many of their men, are run away even at the sight of the enemy . . . I know not the extent of the disaster, but I believe it is very bad.'

Back in mid-October, the Queen had begged Mack von Leiberich, 'General, be to us by land, what my hero, Nelson, has been by sea.' She had also successfully pleaded with Nelson – no matter what occurred – to keep some units of the Royal Navy in the Bay of Naples. He had, of course, complied, and by late November 1798 they were sorely needed on urgent business.

The Kingdom of Naples and the Two Sicilies was ruled in name by Ferdinand IV and in reality by his wife, Maria Carolina, who was sister to the guillotined Marie Antoinette of France.

Naples presented the picture of a city on the edge of anarchy. There were plots among the French-fancying bourgeoisie to capture Sir William and Lady Hamilton, and even Nelson, to hold as hostage. The King's beloved beggars were rising against the bourgeoisie, and preparing to give the French a drubbing.

It was imperative to get the Royal Family, the British-born Prime Minister, Sir Harold Acton, the Hamiltons and other English people out of the city. Nelson concentrated all immediately available men-of-war in the bay.

There were frantic scenes as everyone struggled to convey their possessions (in vast quantities) to the quayside. British armed sailors escorted them and helped them on board. And on 23 December, the *Vanguard*, the most memorable name at that most memorable victory over the French fleet at the Nile, had become no more than a transport for families fleeing the French armies. And her admiral reflected on the corruption and perfidy of Italian troops, and Bavarian generals – and on his own blunder in advocating this fatal military campaign.

ABOVE LEFT The taking of Naples by Bonaparte's army.
BELOW Porta Felice in Palermo, Sicily to where the Royal Family, helped by Nelson and the British fleet, escaped.

Naples was retaken, the Bourbons temporarily re-established. It was for his part in the numerous acts of revenge against the republicans that Nelson was most severely criticized. There was indeed the most horrible bloodbath with the return of King Ferdinand's court to the city. Torture and execution were everyday events, and Nelson himself concurred in the hanging from the yardarm of the republican naval commander, Commodore Francesco Caracciolo, whose court martial took place in his flagship. Caracciolo was with some reason regarded as a traitor, having previously been allied to the Neapolitan court, but it was improper of Nelson not to allow his one-time fellow officer the customary twenty-four hours for prayers and confession before execution. Emma, and the Queen, would not even have given him a trial.

Whatever opprobrium he later suffered for his part in the defence of the Bourbon cause, Nelson was created Duke of Brontë by King Ferdinand, a title he enjoyed as richly as any other, and one he henceforth used on every occasion.

Apart from the capture of *Le Généreux*, the early weeks of the new century brought Nelson no better fortune. Bonaparte had escaped from Egypt, through the blockades off Alexandria at one end of the Mediterranean and Toulon at the other. Malta still held

out, with no evident sustenance. Nelson took the Hamiltons along
to see the blockade, as if it were some fairground sideshow, and in
the hope of seeing the French garrison capitulate. Instead, while
Emma was on the quarterdeck of the *Foudroyant*, a ranging shot
from a French fort struck the ship. Emma refused to go below; she
wanted to watch the fun. Then the flagship's fore-topmast was hit,
and the affronted Nelson had to take his ship out of range. As one
midshipman remarked, 'Lady Hamilton, finding that the French
governor would not surrender until he had made a meal of his shoes,
influenced Lord Nelson to turn his head for Palermo, a much more
agreeable place, and where the balls were not all of iron.'

The decision was made in London that The Hero of The Nile must
return home. Some officials thought he was becoming a diplomatic
embarrassment, others that his vanity, or his love affair, conflicted
with his naval duties so that he had become a liability, and others
that he was tired and sick from long service abroad. All were correct, in some measure.

A vessel was offered to Nelson and his party by Lord Keith. But
Sir William Hamilton had nearly died of seasickness on the brief
voyage from Naples to Palermo. Nor did Emma care for the sea. To
travel overland with the Hamiltons had certain attractions, especially for Emma, who longed to flaunt her famous paramour to the
courts of Europe.

Everywhere acclaim. Everywhere curiosity to see and cheer The Hero of The Nile. Everywhere gossip about the fair, fat, heavy-drinking, heavy-eating, heavy-gambling Emma. And what of her husband, who keeps her in all that diaphanous finery and jewelry? What does he think of this affair between the most famous admiral and most famous courtesan, his wife? The answer is, he does not appear to mind in the least. He certainly could not be on more friendly terms with his wife's paramour.

They were at Vienna for weeks, until 26 September, where they left the Queen and her party behind. After their departure, one notable citizen wrote to his niece about the impression the celebrated lovers made:

> I often found myself in the company of this odd pair, and Lady Hamilton never stopped talking, singing, laughing, gesticulating and mimicking, while the favoured son of Neptune appeared to leave her no more than did her shadow, trying to meet with his own small eyes the great orbs of his beloved, and, withal, as motionless and silent as a monument, embarrassed by his poor figure and by all the emblems, cords and crosses with which he was be-decked. In a word, the Lord of the Nile seemed as clumsy and dim on land as he is adroit and notable at sea.

A hint of officialdom's view of Nelson's recent conduct met him at Hamburg, where it became clear that no Royal Navy vessel was

A detail of a white muslin dress worn by Emma on her return to England; the names of Nelson and Brontë, a Sicilian title given to him by King Ferdinand, were embroidered around the hem in gold thread and sequins.

to be provided for the party's passage to England. Nelson was obliged to charter a packet, which made a stormy early November passage of no fewer than five days to Yarmouth.

Here, in his home county of Norfolk, there were no reservations about what the people thought of their hero. Crowds lined the streets, raced to his carriage and unharnessed the horses to draw it themselves to the Town Hall where the Mayor and Corporation gave him the Freedom of Yarmouth.

At the Wrestler's Inn, where the party was to stay the night, the landlord begged permission to rename his hostelry 'The Nelson Arms'. 'That would be absurd, seeing that I have but one,' retorted Nelson with a laugh. From an upper window, he waved that one arm to the crowds below. Emma stood proprietorially at his side in a muslin gown decorated with flounces and elaborately embroidered with anchors and garlands, acorns and oak leaves, and the words 'Nelson' and 'Brontë'.

Nelson returned to England with the Hamiltons on 6 November 1800, arriving to a tumultuous welcome at Great Yarmouth.

London, Sunday 9 November 1800. It is three o'clock in the afternoon of a dark day, heavy with storm clouds. A hotel off King Street, St James. Here virtuous, anxious Fanny is staying, with her father-in-law. She has heard much – far too much – of Lady Hamilton, directly and not always tactfully from her husband, and more – all unpleasant – on the doubtful winds of gossip. She could not hope to escape it, however circumspect people might be. Those cruel cartoons making fun of her husband, on sale everywhere!

Lady Nelson is forty-two, frail-looking, a little pinched, for if it is not cold, it is winter, and she does not care for the winter. And she has not seen her husband for nearly three years.

Nelson arrives by carriage at the hotel entrance, with his manservant. At his side is Emma Hamilton, her condition concealed by her size and full dress, and Sir William, elderly, so tired, so stooping. And Emma's mother.

Nelson formally greets his wife, turns to make the introductions, and the two women eye one another for the first time. For Fanny there is immediate distrust and constraint. She is too good to hate easily. But beneath the piety there are grave doubts, and deeper anxieties now than ever.

For Emma, bundled up against the winter afternoon in her travelling clothes, there is no embarrassment. It is a scene she has long anticipated, many times rehearsed. She has often in the past

faced the hurt or angry eyes of wronged wives; they are an occu-
pational hazard. For all the fine breeding of Lady Nelson, and her
legal status as her paramour's wife, with society's moral code upon
her side and the friendship and support of Nelson's family, this
woman has failed. She has failed to hold her husband's love, to provide the response to his own passion he so badly needed. Though she
admires, she also frets at her husband's physical courage. She has
even failed to bear the child he longed for. The hero is Emma's in
all but name: in his love and in his bed, he is hers.

That night Nelson spent with his father and wife. It was the last
occasion when he shared a bed with Fanny – if he did share it. One
wonders. Reliable gossip has it that he was up betimes, and out
into St James, to join once again the Hamiltons for breakfast at
Sir William's house in Piccadilly.

It was an impossible situation. Here was the nation's hero back
home in his native land for the first time since the victory of the
Nile. There were official functions daily, receptions, banquets, services of thanksgiving. At the more formal of these it had to be Lord
and Lady Nelson and not Lord Nelson and Lady Hamilton. Protocol
demanded it. Guilt-stricken and anguished, Nelson endured the
presence of a wife whose love and loyalty had never wavered, whose
solicitousness when he had been last at home had been so essential
to the repair of his mental and physical injuries: the deeply religious, conscience-stricken Christian fighting and losing against
infidelity and the passions of the flesh. In the eyes of the world he
might be the hero – and in spite of all his protestations how he loved
it! – but deep in his Christian conscience there lurked the dreadful
word 'Shame!' It would lie there until the day he died.

King George III himself set the tone from Court. A well-known
admirer of Nelson, a keen follower of his campaigns and battles,
yet he refused to receive Emma, and when he met Nelson again for
the first time since the triumph of the Nile, he turned briefly to
enquire after his health, and then pointedly engaged an obscure
army officer in prolonged conversation. Cuthbert Collingwood's
dry comment upon this incident, referring to the Army's poor showing in the war, was, 'It could not be about *his* success.'

On occasions when he had to be seen in company with Fanny,
Nelson's coldness towards her was barely concealed, to the em-
barrassment of hostesses. At an Admiralty House dinner, when
Fanny thoughtfully shelled some walnuts and passed a wine glass

A view of Piccadilly from Hyde Park Corner turnpike.

filled with them across the table, Nelson pushed it aside so roughly there was an accident; and Fanny burst into tears. At the theatre with both her husband and the Hamiltons, Fanny fainted at the public attention her husband gave to Emma, and his neglect of herself.

By the first weeks of 1801 the marriage had virtually ceased to exist. The end was as miserable and damaging as the end of most marriages, the consequences multiplied many times over by the fame of Nelson, the notoriety of his mistress, and the plain niceness and distinction of Fanny. We can see her clearly at this time, her once-pretty face pale and wracked by anxiety, finding easement of her misery only in concern with her own ill-health, which has never been far from her thoughts. She has always felt the cold, even in Bath, her winter retreat from the much worse north-easterlies of Burnham. Now, almost five years before Nelson's death, we see this frail, tragic figure in decline: a woman who was too honest to

111

flatter her husband's vanity when she believed he needed to be
reminded of the need for modesty and propriety; a woman who
counselled caution because she was too tender to relish Nelson's
courage in battle; a woman who could never begin to act the
swashbuckling, blousy, vigorous part of the sensuous *comédienne*
played with such style by Emma Hamilton, which appealed so
strongly to Nelson's earthiness.

There is a reliable account, no doubt filtering down from Fanny

herself, of the final parting between the husband and wife: Lady Nelson in bed, as so often, it seemed. Nelson enters, she puts out a hand which he takes.

Fanny: 'There is not a man in the world who has more honour than you. Now tell me, upon your honour, whether you have ever suspected or heard from anyone anything that renders my own fidelity disputable?'

Nelson: 'No, never.'

Nelson's wife, Fanny, in old age; she outlived him by nearly thirty years.

That is all. 'They then parted', runs the account, 'with natural respect for each other, on all essential points, but their tempers not calculated to suit each other.'

They never saw one another again. But it was not an end of all communication. Before going to sea, he had made financial provision for her, and she acknowledged this gratefully, referring to his 'generosity and tenderness'.

Nelson's last letter does him no credit at all. By this time, he was totally disillusioned in Josiah, who in turn had done his mean worst to bring discredit upon his stepfather and patron, publicly mocking Nelson, and wishing that he would fall as he made his way, clumsily, dangerously up a ladder with one arm.

'I have done *all* for him,' runs Nelson's last report to the young man's mother, 'and he may again, as he has often done before, wish me to break my neck, and be abetted in it by his friends, who are likewise my enemies; but I have done my duty as an honest, generous man, and I neither want nor wish for anybody to care what becomes of me . . .'

Returning now to Fanny, the ink flowed bitterly from his pen. 'Living, I have done all in my power for you, and if dead, you will find I have done the same; therefore my only wish is to be left to myself; and wishing you every happiness, believe that I am, your affectionate Nelson and Brontë.'

In crude contrast, he had written to Emma a few days earlier a letter bursting with passion, claiming how 'susceptible and true' was his heart, which had never loved anyone else but her.

> My longing for you, both person and conversation, you may readily imagine. What must be my sensations at the idea of sleeping with you! it setts me on fire, even the thoughts, much more would the reality. I am sure my love & desires are all to you, and if any woman naked were to come to me, even as I am this moment from thinking of you, I hope it might rot off if I would touch her even with my hand. No, my heart, person and mind is in perfect union of love towards my own, dear beloved Emma.

Still Fanny could not accept the reality of her 'dismissal' and 'the silence you have imposed'. She wrote without response several more short notes, and then just before Christmas 1801, for the last time, referring to the comfortable, warm house she had to offer him. 'Do, my dear husband, let us live together. I can never be happy till such an event takes place. I assure you again I have but one wish in the world, to please you. Let everything be buried in oblivion, it will pass away like a dream.'

Alas! she learned to regret the words. The letter came back marked: 'Opened by mistake by Lord Nelson, but not read'.

Fanny lived to the age of seventy-three, but always, it appeared, in weak health. There is a brief, characteristic glimpse of her shortly before Nelson's death, a figure lying on a sofa in the home of a friend. She raised herself to her feet when a guest entered the room, and made her way to the door 'with a lameness like a sprain, by her manner of walking.' 'Poor creature,' this eyewitness recorded, 'I felt ashamed of my red eyes for *tiny* sorrows in comparison with hers, and longed to support her down the stairs.'

6

'I Do not See the Signal'

Nelson hoisted his flag again on 17 January 1801. He had left behind him numerous likenesses for posterity, not all of them flattering. The cartoonists had been busy on him, on Lady Hamilton, and the two of them together – Gillray was the most famous and sharpest. Apart from these unwanted caricatures, Nelson was prevailed upon to sit for some of the most famous portraitists of his day. He found time to visit John Hoppner's studio, he was sketched by the Dutchman Simon de Koster, sat for a bust by Mrs Anne Damer. 'That foolish little fellow', commented Lord St Vincent, who never minced his words, 'has sat to every artist in London.'

Perhaps a 'foolish little fellow' on land, by St Vincent's reckoning. At sea, and at war, his judgment of Nelson remained as high as ever, and it was to his flag that Nelson attached himself at Portsmouth that January. He was relieved to be free of the complexities of life ashore – public snubs one day, the cheering crowds as he was granted the freedom of some city the next – and desperately keen to be away: his cup of happiness he shared with his mistress was now brimming as he heard the news that she had given birth safely to the child they had conceived on board the *Foudroyant*. A girl. Horatia, Emma wanted to call her. Nelson did not demur.

Lord St Vincent received Nelson gladly. Had they not shared so much war, with such resounding success? But the old admiral understood his second-in-command's weaknesses as well as his strengths, and noted wryly that Nelson 'appeared and acted as if he had done me an injury, and felt apprehensive that I was acquainted with it. Poor man! He is devoured with vanity, weakness and folly; was stuck with ribbons, medals, etc. and yet pretended that he wished to avoid the honour and ceremony he everywhere met with upon the road.'

A painting by Fuger of the confident, mature Nelson in 1800; Nelson always liked to be painted wearing his smart uniforms and bedecked with his colourful decorations.

However, the team was to be broken up before they could even put to sea again. And for the first time, after years in American and Mediterranean waters, Nelson was to sail east into the ·Baltic. Britain's troubles had been made even more grievous by the revival of an old alliance, the Armed Neutrality of the North between Russia, Sweden, Prussia and Denmark, which included Norway. This not only threatened Britain's blockade of France; it threatened to cut off her vital trade with the Baltic powers, which included the timber and other raw materials essential for maintaining her supremacy at sea.

Prime Minister Pitt favoured an armed demonstration in the Baltic, and if necessary a pre-emptive strike to demonstrate British naval paramountcy.

Nelson wrote to Emma that he had just received 'an order to hoist my flag in the *St George*, as Lord Spencer says I must go forth as the Champion of England in the north'. However, his first difficulty was to 'go forth' at all. It was not to be his expedition; he was to be second-in-command again, this time to an admiral who had been most critical of Nelson's insubordinate behaviour to Keith in the Mediterranean.

Sir Hyde Parker, who was notoriously slow and fumbling, was a portly, self-indulgent sixty-two-year-old admiral with an undistinguished but not wholly unsuccessful service record. He had first gone to sea eight years before Nelson was born. He had recently married a bride of eighteen – 'batter pudding' was St Vincent's pithy comment on her. There is no record of his reaction to the news from the Admiralty that the hero, this hurricane of a fire-eater who laid down his own laws as readily as he laid alongside the enemy, was to be his second-in-command. That he did not approve is self-evident. That his reception of Nelson at Yarmouth, where his first concern was the details of a great ball for his bride, was chilly, was witnessed by all present. Nelson was pointedly excluded from planning conferences.

What a contrast with Nelson's arrival only five months earlier at Yarmouth! Nelson nagged, wrote letters of complaint to the Admiralty, observed the slackness everywhere in Parker's fleet. The man never even slept in his flagship, so what could you expect? 'Consider how nice it must be laying in bed with a young wife, compared to a damned cold raw wind,' Nelson wrote bitterly to his old friend Troubridge, now at the Admiralty.

ABOVE William Pitt sketched in 1789 by James Gillray; Nelson much admired Pitt who led England in the war against France during most of the 1790s until his death in 1806.
BELOW Admiral Sir Hyde Parker.

Ah where, & ah where, is my gallant Sailor gone?
He's gone to Fight the Frenchmen for George upon the Throne } *DIDO, in Despair!* { *He's gone to fight ye Frenchmen, t'loose t'other Arm & Eye*
And left me with the old Antique, to lay me down & Cry.

ABOVE A cartoon by James Gillray called 'Dido in Despair'; Nelson put to sea again in January 1801 when Emma was nine months pregnant by him; note Sir William Hamilton asleep in the bed beside Emma, with his broken antiquities on the floor; Nelson, a frequent visitor to Emma's bedroom, has left his sash behind on the floor.

A damned cold raw wind it was, too, when at last lethargic old Parker was prevailed upon to put to sea, his fleet at once demonstrating its slackness with poor station keeping. There were 11 ships of the line, 11 frigates, and a host of brigs and fireships, cutters and sloops – 53 sail in all.

Three of the four nations in the Confederation might have insane rulers – Russia a dangerously mad Tsar – the only exception being Prussia, which had a ruler of equal lethargy and indecisiveness to Admiral Parker's, and no fleet at all. However, these Baltic powers could put to sea a combined fleet of more than twice the power of the British Fleet, and this consideration caused Parker to exercise even greater caution, to the point of timidity.

After a savagely cold crossing of the North Sea, to Nelson's chagrin Parker ordered the fleet to anchor eighteen miles from Kronborg and Elsinore (Helsingør), although there was a fair wind for Copenhagen. Nelson had seen a frigate detached and had rightly guessed that she carried a diplomat for conducting peaceful

119

negotiations. 'I hate your pen and ink men,' commented the victor of the Nile who had signalled 'Close action!' on sighting the enemy, and no more had been necessary. Negotiations indeed!

A frustrated officer who was only a firebrand, and no more, might have reacted violently. Nelson knew better, and tried charm. Instead of an angry note to the flagship, Nelson composed a delicate and charming one to accompany a gift of what he had learned Parker had a fancy for: a fine turbot recently landed by one of his lieutenants. The reaction was all that Nelson could hope for, even if it did not raise Parker in his estimation. A courteous note of thanks was soon received, and later an invitation to participate in the consultations on board the flagship. The planning was now purely warlike. The negotiations had failed, as Nelson knew they would. 'Now we are sure of fighting, I am sent for,' he noted sharply. 'When it was a joke, I was kept in the background.'

Not that Nelson approved of consultations as such. On the contrary, 'If a man consults whether he is to fight, when he has the power in his own hands, *it is certain that his opinion is against fighting.*' Again, it was as he feared. Procrastination and uncertainty prevailed, and Nelson knew that delay was the greatest enemy: delay allowing the Danes to prepare their defences, concentrate their forces, perhaps come out with a combined force the English could never match. Hearing from the failed diplomat the nature of the enemy's defences (especially the shore defences of powerful batteries that made the French at Aboukir Bay seem like peashooters), Nelson had contrived and outlined a plan to take the anchored Danish fleet from the south, requiring a difficult and dangerous passage of the Belt instead of the Sound – 'the *home* stroke' he called it.

Nothing had been decided. On returning to his flagship, Nelson descended to his cabin and, in the spidery writing that would never match the neatness of his right hand, penned a final appeal to his superior. 'The more I have reflected, the more I am confirmed in opinion, that not a moment should be lost in attacking the Enemy . . . Here you are', he appealed, 'with almost the safety, certainly with the honour, of England more entrusted to you than ever yet fell to the lot of any British Officer . . . I am of opinion the boldest measures are the safest; and our Country demands a most vigorous exertion of her force, directed with judgement.'

The advice could scarcely have been more pointed; and with

The British fleet passing Elsinore on 30 March 1801 on its way through the Baltic Sound to Copenhagen.

some self-satisfaction, he now wrote to Emma: 'Sir Hyde Parker has by this time found out the worth of your Nelson, and that he is a useful sort of man on a pinch; therefore, if he has ever thought unkindly of me, I freely forgive him. Nelson must stand among the first, or he must fall.'

At last, on 26 March, Nelson received the orders he had been expecting. He was to do the fighting, of course. He was to take 10 sail of the line, 4 frigates, 4 sloops, 7 bombs, 2 fireships and 12 gun brigs, and approach Copenhagen and the Danish fleet by way of the Sound, the Belt being considered too risky by Parker. ('I don't care

121

a damn by which passage we go,' commented Nelson in exasperation, 'so that we fight them.') There was to be a bombardment and, if appropriate, a landing by the 49th Regiment, which had been embarked at Yarmouth.

An evening reconnaissance in a schooner confirmed all Nelson's worst fears. The batteries had been greatly strengthened, the defending ships reinforced, all navigation buoys removed. Every preparation had been made to defend the harbour and the city, and it soon became evident that the Swedes and Russians were present in strength, too. 'The more numerous the better, I wish they were twice as many,' Nelson was heard to remark in a determined effort to maintain the spirit of optimism and determination of his officers. 'The easier the victory, depend on it.'

The spirit of the fleet had now been transformed by Nelson; never had the spirit of the Band of Brothers been so high; never had the need for their unique blend of loyalty, warlike prowess, courage and leadership been so necessary. On 1 April 1801 Nelson, his flag now in the shallow-draught *Elephant*, passed Copenhagen with his eleven ships (Parker had generously reinforced him with two more), frigates and the rest, and anchored unmolested to the south of a shoal called the Middle Ground. The timing of the attack now depended on the wind.

After dark, Nelson summoned his captains to the flagship for a final briefing and a toast to a victory every one of them *knew* would be theirs. The senior army officer present, Lieutenant-Colonel the Hon. William Stewart, afterwards wrote of 'the gallant Nelson' sitting down to table 'with a large party of his comrades in arms. He was in the highest spirits, and drank to a leading wind, and to the success of the ensuing day. Every man separated with feelings of admiration for their great leader, and with anxious impatience to follow him to the approaching Battle.'

Obliged by sheer weariness to take to his cot, Nelson still scarcely slept that night, calling for his clerks, dictating further instructions, enquiring about the weather. Before the attack could begin, the wind must swing to the north. With daybreak, it was observed that it had indeed swung through 180 degrees, like a finger beckoning the British fleet into action. Nelson needed no such encouragement; but he could observe again that fortune favours the brave, that the God of War was on his side, that all the omens were good.

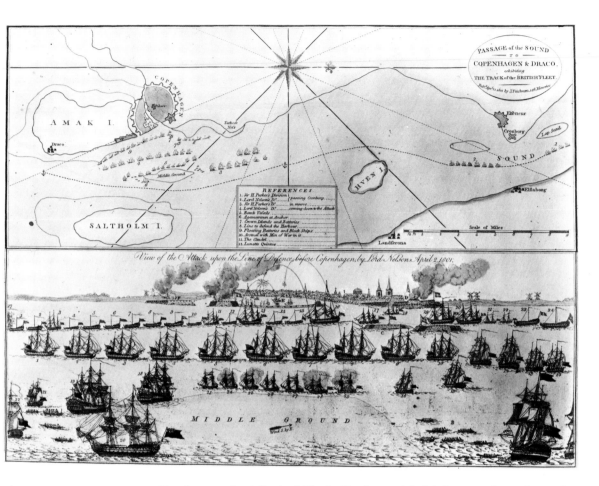

A contemporary map showing the position of the British fleet at the Battle of Copenhagen on 2 April 1801.

To the north, Admiral Hyde Parker with his heavy, deep-draught ships, observed Nelson's squadron sailing slowly into battle, the *Edgar*, *Ardent* and *Glatton* in the van, the *Elephant* flying Nelson's flag midway in the line, and the rest. In their failure (a word he allowed upon his lips) or success his reputation was staked. And he had never before felt so uneasy. But neither had he ever fought with Nelson, and was quite unwarmed by the fire of battle that was inspiring the Band of Brothers eagerly facing combat four miles away. His mind was upon the massive strength of the Danish batteries: the Trekroner fort alone powerful enough to disable every one of his subordinate's vessels, in his estimate.

All Parker's forebodings appeared to be justified in the opening minutes of the attack. Nelson's ships were unable to take up their stations alongside the anchored enemy line. His old ship *Agamemnon* had evidently run aground, and like the *Culloden* at the Nile

123

took no part in the fight, in which her absence was sorely felt. To Parker, confusion appeared to reign in the English line even before the first guns spoke.

The opening phase was just as disastrous as the Commander-in-Chief believed it to be. In spite of the reinstatement of some of the buoys by intrepid boats' crews working in the darkness, and the presence of pressed pilots who were supposed to know the tricky waters of Copenhagen roads, two more of Nelson's ships ran aground, the second mistakenly following the first in the smoke and confusion of battle.

When news of this disaster was transmitted to the *Elephant*, Nelson's Flag-Captain (Foley, of Nile fame) reprimanded the officer delivering the message, not for its contents but for the wording and tone in which it was conveyed. Quite right, confirmed Nelson. 'I think at such a moment, the delivery of anything like a desponding opinion, unasked, was highly reprehensible.'

Dispositions had been rearranged by hastily hoisted signals, no captain had panicked or lost his nerve in these critical minutes.

ABOVE The Battle of Copenhagen was a slogging gunfight between the two opposing lines; the anchored Danish fleet are on the right.

124

With only the yellow pricks of muzzle flashes in the smoke to mark the position of many of the ships, the British ships of the line anchored close alongside the enemy, or engaged the great forts in unequal combat; and what was to become known as the Battle of Copenhagen became a slogging gun duel in which nerve and gunnery speed were to be the arbiters.

For almost three hours, the British gun crews, fastest in the world, spurred on by the officers, continued an unbroken cannonade: broadside following broadside, the great guns plunging back in recoil, men shouting and falling, powder monkeys darting with their lethal burdens, sliding down the vertical pole through deck after deck to the magazines deep in the bowels of the ship. Ball against thick solid wood, or stone ramparts – it was slow going, demanding prodigies of strength and spirit.

Hyde Parker was attempting to approach the battle through the billowing clouds of smoke rolling towards him. But the contrary wind allowed him little progress. He was also seized with fear and indecision. The continuing fire of the forts and the Danish ships convinced him that, this time, Nelson had taken on odds he could never hope to unbalance.

He wished Nelson would withdraw, having done his best, but he

BELOW A Danish engraving showing how close to Copenhagen the battle was fought.

This study of Nelson was painted by Sir William Beechey during the few months spent by Nelson in England before the Battle of Copenhagen; the wound inflicted over Nelson's right eye at the Battle of the Nile can be seen clearly; the artist has painted Nelson's eyes brown instead of grey.

was fearful of ordering him to do so. He was, indeed, fearful of doing anything. In the end, soon after one o'clock, he seemed set on a compromise solution. Tom Southey, brother of the poet who became an early Nelson biographer, overheard the old admiral say, 'I will make the signal for recall for Nelson's sake. If he is in a condition to continue the action successfully, he will disregard it; if he is not, it will be an excuse for his retreat, and no blame can be imputed to him.' How little did he understand his subordinate!

He was prevailed upon to delay hoisting this signal for perhaps another twenty minutes. Then at half past one, still seeing no end to the battle, no end to the Danish resistance, Parker decided that

Nelson must be recalled at all costs. 'The fire is too hot for him to oppose. A retreat must be made . . .'

Nelson was pacing the starboard side of his quarterdeck, a select party at his side. The *Elephant* was firing at the Danish flagship, *Dannebrog*, and at two floating batteries that were giving a great deal of trouble. Splinters from a ball that had struck the mainmast above fell to the deck about him. 'This is warm work,' Colonel Stewart heard him say with some relish. The admiral paused at the gangway, looking about him at the smoke and bloody confusion: the litter-strewn waters of Copenhagen roads, the dead in the water, the wounded crying out, the stabs of gunfire that seemed to come from every quarter of the compass.

The signal lieutenant approached Nelson as he resumed his pacing, and reported Signal 39 – Discontinue Action – received from the flagship. Nelson gave no sign of hearing, and merely continued his rapid, impatient walking. As he came back at the end of his turn, the lieutenant asked, 'Shall I repeat the signal, Sir?'

This time, Nelson answered crisply, 'No, acknowledge it.'

The lieutenant saluted, and made for the poop. He turned when he heard his Admiral's voice calling out above the thunder of gunfire, 'Is Number 16 [for close action] still hoisted?'

'Yes, Sir, it is.'

'Mind you keep it so.'

Nelson once again resumed his walking, according to Stewart noticeably agitated, his state of mind reflected in the purposeless waving of his stump. The officers remained silent for a turn or two. Then Nelson suddenly came out, as if exclaiming the impossible, 'Do you know what's shown on board of the Commander-in-Chief? Number 39!'

'What, Sir, does that mean?' asked the army officer, ignorant of the mysteries of maritime signalling.

'Why, to leave off action. Leave off action!' It was like an expletive. Nelson shrugged his shoulders. 'Now damn me if I do!' He turned to his flag-captain. 'You know, Foley, I have only one eye – I have a right to be blind sometimes.'

Nelson took the glass from under his left arm and raised it theatrically to his blind eye. In a voice which might have been that of his father, who so loved a joke, he said, 'I do not see the signal.'

The Trekroner fort especially was still doing great damage. Every time a man fell at the guns, another took his place from the

An aquatint showing
the final destruction
of the Danish fleet.

unlimited reserves. That bold frigate captain, Edward Riou (beloved by all, in Society and at sea), lost his clerk at his side as he
planted himself on the barrel of a gun further to urge on his men.
Another ball took away a party of marines. 'Come, then, my boys,
let us all die together!' cried this gallant officer; and was almost at
once cut in two by another shot.

But at last, by two o'clock, it seemed as if British gunnery was
prevailing. The forts were still busy, but hardly a shot now came
from the Danish line of ships, many of which were in a terrible condition. As at the Nile, the most dramatic end was reserved for the
enemy flagship. The *Dannebrog* had struck her colours but could
not be boarded because she had broken her moorings, and burning
furiously, was drifting before the wind, causing terror among her
consorts, and among her surviving crew, who threw themselves
into the water from gun ports on every deck. Uncertain of her
identity, the shore batteries opened fire on the ship, adding to the
suffering, until she mercifully blew up at half past three.

The fact that the Danish fleet was beaten was understood by only
a handful of people outside the battle. Some of the Danish ships had
not even been engaged. Others were a shambles, but as soon as the
colours were lowered, some brave body would climb aloft and

rehoist them, to the fury of the British. The Trekroner fort, on the other hand, was still capable of driving off any ship of the line.

Nelson knew for certain that the day was his, and his compassionate heart was in agony at the unnecessary carnage taking place all about him.

'To the Brothers of Englishmen, the Danes,' he began his urgent message, penned awkwardly but with a steady left hand on deck and amid the fire of battle: 'Lord Nelson has directions to spare Denmark, when no longer resisting; but if the firing is continued on the part of Denmark, Lord Nelson will be obliged to set on fire all the floating-batteries he has taken, without having the power of saving the brave Danes who have defended them. Dated on board his Britannic Majesty's Ship *Elephant*, Copenhagen Roads, April 2nd 1801.'

And signed it with his usual flourish – 'Nelson and Brontë, Vice-Admiral, under the Command of Admiral Sir Hyde Parker.'

Victory was once again complete. As Nelson himself recorded: 'April 2. Moderate breezes southerly. At 9 [actually 10] made the

A set of china, showing Nelson's arms, made to commemorate the Battle of Copenhagen; the manufacturers made an error with the date of the battle as it in fact took place on 2 April.

After the battle, Nelson was sent ashore to conclude an armistice with the Regent of Denmark.

signal to engage the Danish line; the action began at 5 min. and lasted about 4 hours, when 17 out of 18 of the Danish line were taken, burnt or sunk. Our ships suffered a good deal . . .'

If the Danes had known just how badly the British ships had suffered, with nearly 1,000 dead, they might have counter-attacked with fresh ships previously uninvolved in the battle. But they were stunned equally by the cannonade, and the moral impact of their famous opponent, and appalled by their own losses of men (some 6,000) and men-of-war.

Nelson reported to his supine Commander-in-Chief, who, whatever his true feelings, could only offer his subordinate congratulations on his unaided victory. Never, claimed the admiral, were Nelson's exertions 'carried to a higher pitch of zeal for his Country's service'. An armistice was concluded, and Nelson was asked by Parker to go ashore and negotiate with Frederick, Crown Prince and Regent of Denmark – as if he had not already worked enough to bring about this overwhelming victory.

From fighting admiral, to diplomatist – and then, still without rest though complaining of feeling 'very unwell', to the role of compassionate visitor: he had himself rowed in his gig about his battered squadron to enquire after the dead and bring cheer to the wounded, like Tom Southey, and Captain Tom Thompson who had lost a leg, and to congratulate all on their sterling work.

By a cruel and ironical stroke of fate, the mad Tsar Paul of Russia was assassinated a few days after the victory. As he had been the instigator of the Treaty of Armed Neutrality, and was succeeded by a moderate liberal who at once reversed the pro-French policy, it can be said that Copenhagen need never have been fought. Certainly, it had none of the profound strategic consequences of the Battle of the Nile. Nor did it have the same emotional impact on the British people. There was no war with the Danes, no hatred against them. It had just been a necessary pre-emptive strike.

Lord St Vincent, now First Lord of the Admiralty, wrote extravagantly, 'It does not become me to make comparisons: all agree there is but one Nelson. That he may long continue the pride of his Country is the fervent wish of your Lordship's truly affectionate St Vincent.' There was no shortage of professional praise; his Band of Brothers loved and admired him more deeply than ever. As a professional victory it at least equalled the Nile, and the Danes had been a much more intractable foe than the French.

But it was not only weariness that caused Nelson to be seized with a sense of bitterness at the lack of public and official response to his victory. Marks of thanks were conspicuously missing: no sovereign's gold medals for his captains as for the Nile, and precious little prize money either. A viscountcy for himself, it was true, but no earldom, as St Vincent had been created.

And when Nelson went to pay his respects to King George, he was asked whether he had left port since their last meeting. 'Lord Nelson, do you get out?'

'I was tempted to say,' Nelson reported later, ' "Sir, I have been out and am come in again. Your Majesty perhaps has not heard of the Battle of Copenhagen!"'

It is an irony of Nelson's life, and of history, that all four of his great victories – at Cape St Vincent, the Nile, Copenhagen and Trafalgar – were succeeded by disasters or follies: Tenerife after the first, then the unsuccessful Neapolitan campaign; and now Boulogne.

Nelson's seal.

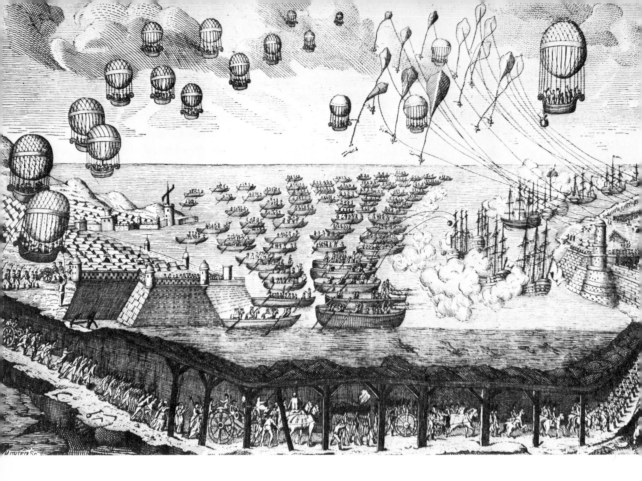

The threat of invasion was rarely out of men's minds during Bonaparte's years of conquest, and the removal of danger from the Baltic by the victory at Copenhagen and the death of the mad Tsar did not diminish it. In the summer of 1801, there were said to be no fewer than 36 gun sloops, more than 200 gunboats and many more smaller vessels, especially flat-bottom boats for troop-carrying, in the French-controlled ports from Flushing to Cherbourg. Agents told of 40,000 of Bonaparte's troops encamped and ready to sail.

An officer of skill, experience and determination was required to protect English shores from Suffolk to Sussex, someone whose name would put steel into the spirits of Englishmen for whom 'Boney' had become a bogeyman. Lord St Vincent had amused and reassured Englishmen by his statement that he did not say that the French could not come: 'I only say that they cannot come by sea.' But a man of Nelson's fame and stature was required for the present task.

His appointment to this special command suited him admirably, offering the opportunity to get away to sea while spending what time he could spare with the Hamiltons.

Nelson immediately began a series of provocative strikes, with

his squadron of small ships fitted to the task, against shipping off French ports. The first, on 4 August 1801, was observed in clear weather by a jubilant crowd assembled on the cliffs above Dover. They had come to hear 'Nelson speaking to the French', and had the satisfaction of witnessing 'the Nelson touch' in action without any danger to themselves. Five French vessels were sent to the bottom or driven ashore, and more damaged.

But this, according to Nelson, had been a trifling affair, and he let it be widely known that he had larger, more substantial plans in mind, this time a full-scale assault on Boulogne to destroy all threat from the French flotillas and the military forces intended to sail in them. Nelson conceived the operation in terms of a naval battle similar to the Nile and Copenhagen, the British light forces – gunboats, ketches, bombships and specially constructed landing craft – proceeding from one group of vessels to the next, 'a sufficient number being left to guard the prize, the others are immediately to pursue the object by proceeding on to the next, and so on until the whole of the Flotilla be either taken or totally annihilated . . .' So ran the instructions for a strike he left to others to carry out.

The French had plenty of warning, had chained their vessels firmly to the shore, sited the defences cleverly. The attack was a bloody fiasco, and was driven off with heavy casualties, including one of Nelson's closest friends mortally wounded: 'I beg his hair may be cut off and given to me,' pleaded Nelson with the surgeon. 'It shall remain and be buried with me.'

Nelson let it be known that things would have gone differently if he had led the attack; and the general public were inclined to agree, so that his reputation remained untarnished. It was providential that he had remained in England, for there is every likelihood that he would not have returned.

In the complex world of politics and the balance of European

An English assault on Boulogne was a total failure and resulted in a heavy loss of life.

The Peace of Amiens being proclaimed at the Royal Exchange in London in 1802.

power, an uneasy peace between Britain and France appeared imminent by 14 October 1801, when Nelson wrote to the Admiralty 'to request that Their Lordships will, when they think the service will admit of it, allow me permission to go on shore'. When the Peace of Amiens was finally signed in March 1802, Nelson was among those patriots who deplored the savage French terms, which deprived Britain of almost all her recently acquired Dutch, Spanish and French possessions, and demanded her withdrawal from the island of Malta.

In spite of the inaction forced upon him by this unaccustomed peace in Europe, Nelson found personal happiness in the months ahead, when the curious (and publicly notorious) *ménage à trois* he had formed with the Hamiltons settled into a state of domestic bliss – at least for two of them.

The romantic in Nelson had always dreamed of a country retreat, a country seat where he could harvest the just rewards of his arduous years at sea – a 'paradise', a 'farm', where he could breed stock, till the soil, enjoy the pursuits of a gentleman of substance at leisure, entertaining his friends and, like his dear friend Sir William, dabbling in the arts.

Emma, ever alert to the romantic dreams of her paramour, and fancying the picture of herself in this bucolic setting, had purchased a property in Surrey, near enough to the capital for convenience, near enough to the Portsmouth Road to communicate with Britain's premier naval base. Merton Place it was called, in highly fashionable Twickenham, and Emma had paid £9,000 for it

on his behalf, when Nelson could command no more than £3,000 (a
loan was forthcoming).

'Paradise Merton', as it came to be called in the family, was a
moderate-sized red-brick mansion on two floors, built about a hundred years earlier, with a modest lodge and drive, a well-stocked
garden, a branch of the River Wandle running through land whose
area can be judged by Sir William's comment, 'You have a good
mile of pleasant dry walk around your own farm'.

Nelson first set eyes upon his estate on 23 October 1801, when he
arrived in a chaise-and-four in the village of Merton. The locals had
set up a triumphal arch for the hero, their new, celebrated neighbour, and everyone was out to greet and to cheer him. It was a pre-
cursor of what Merton Place was to become – a temple of honour to
its owner. Here, alongside the fine works of art of Sir William
Hamilton, were placed mementoes and trophies of Nelson's campaigns and battles, from ships' models and battle flags, to paintings
of himself and enemy ships he had captured and destroyed (*L'Orient*
blowing up prominently hung), facsimiles of his honours and
awards. In the hall stood the topmast of the French flagship at the

Nile, and 'an excellent marble bust of the illustrious Admiral', as one visitor described it. Outside, even the muddy stream was renamed 'The Nile'. Everything, it seemed, was intended as a reminder to visitors of the achievements and fame of the people of Merton's new neighbour.

From Merton, Nelson would frequently make the one-hour journey to the Admiralty, and to the office of Lord St Vincent, who was as gruffly disapproving of Nelson's *ménage*, and neglect of his wife, as some of his Band of Brothers, notably Hardy, who never minced his words and retained a strong admiration and affection for poor Fanny.

Emma might never be received at Court, but at Merton the famous threesome were accepted by all, and there was a constant flow of visitors, and dinners for fourteen on most nights. Here at Merton, Nelson basked alike in the affection and attentive care of Emma, the friendship of Sir William and the adulation of all those who came up the avenue of close-planted trees and shrubs. In the way that only Nelson could achieve, the 'Paradise' dream had become a reality.

Time had blunted the guilt and shame over Fanny which had once cut so deep. The conscience and loyalty to Fanny of his family suffered a change, too, with the passage of time. At first Nelson's father had remained stoutly loyal to the daughter-in-law with whom he had a special and close relationship, and sternly disapproving of his son's adulterous relationship. But gradually he found the social attractions of Merton too strong, the reflected glory of his famous son and the charm and flattery of Emma too beguiling to resist. Muttering that he would of course be compelled 'sometimes to be with Lady Nelson' he also wrote that he must become one of the inhabitants of the 'Mansion of Peace'. 'Sir William and I are both old men, and we will witness the hero's felicity in retirement,' he wrote in October 1801.

Mercifully for Fanny, she was saved the knowledge of this intended defection of the old man with whom she had shared a roof for all those years of Nelson's absence, for he became fatally ill before the move to Merton, and died at Bath in April 1802.

Others in the family were more precipitate in their switch of loyalty from the sad, disappointed figure of Fanny to the dazzle of Emma's court at Merton Place. Nelson's brother William, a parson for many years now, made no bones about his admiration for Emma

FACING PAGE Thomas Baxter's sketches of life at Merton Place: (above) Emma was a compulsive gambler and had many card parties at Merton to indulge in her favourite hobby; (below left) Emma with Nelson's niece, Charlotte, aged fifteen; (below right) Horace Nelson, Nelson's nephew and heir, is shown on the left of the group; Nelson hoped that his nephew would marry his daughter Horatia but he died of typhoid in 1806.

and his despising of the rejected Fanny. More than once he was heard to use the nicknames 'Tom Tit' and 'the Cub' when referring to Fanny and Josiah.

Many people wondered at Sir William's role, and his feelings, in the Merton *ménage*. Clearly, the old man was philosophical about his lot, and no doubt was glad of the company of Nelson in the household, and glad of the happiness he brought to his wife. There may have been times when he saw himself too uncomfortably in the role of the cuckold, and certainly he suffered many anxieties about Emma's abiding extravagance. His attitude is best summed up in a letter he wrote in January 1802:

> It is but reasonable, after having fagged all my life, that my last days should pass off comfortably & quietly. Nothing at present disturbs me but my debt, and the nonsense I am obliged to submit to here without coming to an explosion, which would be attended with many disagreeable effects, and would totally destroy the comfort of the best man and the best friend I have in the world.

As time went by, and the lavish dinner parties at Merton became more irksome, Sir William came nearest to uttering a *cri de coeur* in a letter written to Emma but composed as if to his nephew and heir, Charles Greville: 'I have no complaint to make, but I feel that the whole attention of my wife is given to Lord N. and his interest in Merton.' As it was this same Charles Greville who had 'given' Emma to Sir William, there is also a certain element of irony in this utterance!

In 1802, in the last summer of peace for so many years, the *ménage à trois* embarked on a long-planned tour of the West Country, including Sir William's estates, which were bringing in a much-needed £5,000 per annum. Rapturous receptions everywhere. More entries to towns through triumphal arches. More and yet more cheering crowds and mayoral celebrations. 'Rule Britannia' when they went to the theatre. The strewing of the hero's path with flowers by young maidens. Cheers from the assembled employees at manufactories. Special fairs, special rowing matches, even a special cattle show. Nelson was 'exhilarated' by it all. So overwhelming and memorable was his reception at Monmouth that it was later celebrated by the establishment of a fine Nelson museum that can be appreciated today. Emma gave entertainments at parties which were said to 'enrapture the whole company', her songs rendered 'with her usual scientific taste and superior vocal excellence'.

It was as great and lavish and vainglorious a progress as the one across Europe in '98. But Sir William was now four years older, and he was very tired at the end as he glumly noted the cost of the trip at close to £500. But, gentleman to the last, he determined that there should be as little unpleasantness as possible to tarnish the relationship which his death must end before long. He detached himself more and more from Merton now, living mainly in his London house, visiting museums, attending his clubs, meetings of the Royal Society, and the sale rooms. 'Let us bear and forbear for God's sake,' was the heart of a long and appealing message to Emma.

By March 1803 the most famous *ménage* in Europe was close to its end. Sir William retired finally to London, fearing that his death at Merton might 'render it an insupportable future abode to the feelings of his tender and illustrious friend'. He died on 6 April 1803, in the arms of the woman he had made famous, his hands held by the left hand of the hero.

Sir William Hamilton's death coincided with the last days of peace with France. Within five weeks of his burial, the Merton

141

A sketch by Thomas Baxter showing Emma in one of her Attitudes at Merton.

ménage was reduced again, to the solitary, sorrowing figure of Emma alone. Two days before the declaration of war, Nelson was appointed to the Mediterranean command; and from this time all was watching and waiting and war as the shape of the hero's life assumed a configuration of impressive grandeur crowned, like the summit of some giant memorial, by the ultimate victory at Trafalgar.

The strategical problem for Britain was what it had so often been in the past, and was to be in the future; the problem of a maritime power, a densely populated island dependent first upon trade for its life, and ultimately dependent, through its naval power, upon the protection of that trade and the island kingdom from invasion. It had been the same in the Dutch Wars of the seventeenth century, and was to be the same again in 1914 and 1939.

The tactical problem was what it had been in 1797, the blockading of France, and later Spain, and the prevention of their two fleets from uniting to form a force so great that it would be beyond the power of the Royal Navy to destroy it. This failure could lead only to invasion.

Britain was a maritime power, not a land power. For Bonaparte, as for Kaiser Wilhelm II a century later, a navy was not a life-saving necessity. For Britain, naval supremacy was a shield of survival. But if St Vincent should be proved wrong, and the enemy *could come by sea*, it was the end of Britain as an independent nation.

Viewed from Whitehall, and on paper, the strategical and tactical demands were as simple as that. At sea, the realities of blockade and interception were more complicated and immensely arduous. They meant for many men, and for years rather than months, the rigours of keeping station off enemy bases, pitching and heaving through interminable winter gales, or in the debilitating heat of a Mediterranean summer. 'We have a uniform sameness,' Nelson once wrote to the Duke of Clarence, 'day after day, and month after month – gales of wind for ever.' And every man had to be kept occupied, fit, fed and happy. It was a *tour de force* of patience and discipline.

Tacking and wearing, under storm canvas or hove to in a calm, these great vessels remained on station. The captains' tasks and responsibilities were burdensome in the extreme, and it is no wonder that many were worn out by it. It is one thing to keep up the spirits and fighting prowess of your men before imminent battle; quite another consideration with the changing seasons, and inaction with no prospect of prize money for a year, two years . . .

It has been left to an American naval historian, Alfred Thayer Mahan, to summarize succinctly the situation at sea in the Napoleonic Wars, when those British 'far-distant, storm-beaten ships, upon which the Grand Army never looked, stood between it and the dominion of the world'.

Nelson appreciated better than ever before the simple reality of national survival in 1803. Whatever ridicule he attracted with his half-comic, half-vainglorious style at Merton, with his weighty mistress, he could – on the professional level – comprehend the pull of power and conquest in world history, and the world in which he lived, as comprehensively and clearly as Pitt himself.

Nelson was a trifle deaf, like many survivors of fleet actions, half-blind in his damaged eyesight, wholly blind to the figure he cut in public with Lady Hamilton, yet his mind was at the height of its power, matured by reflection and discussion in two years ashore as a major figure both in the House of Lords and the Admiralty. The fighting sailor, with unequalled panache, courage and quality of leadership, for whom victory at sea had become as predictable as the sun's ascent to its meridian, had matured into a statesman-warrior of unequalled weight, quality and value to the nation.

The Last Battle

HMS *Victory* today remains a living memorial to the great days of Britain's sailing navy, and to her most famous admiral. Before Nelson, other famous admirals had flown their flag in this ship: Augustus Keppel at the Battle of Ushant, Richard Kempenfelt, Lords Howe and Hood, and of course St Vincent at the battle that had earned him his title.

The *Victory*, the fifth ship to carry this name, had been laid down at Chatham in 1759 as a three-decker of 2,162 tons. She always had a high reputation as a fast sailer, and had been a flagship all her active life. When Nelson hoisted his flag in her in May 1803 she had just completed a radical refit.

As flag-captain, Nelson had his old friend Hardy, the officers were hand-picked, as experienced a Band of Brothers as could be found anywhere, and the warrant officers and lower deck possessed an exceptional *esprit de corps*. With her 100 guns served by some 600 of the finest gunners, she was unsurpassed anywhere in the world as a fighting ship.

The *Victory*, then, was in every respect a worthy ship to carry Nelson's flag, and to bring about what her Admiral, with economy and simplicity, described as his 'first object': 'To keep the French Fleet in check: and if they put to sea, to have force enough with me to *annihilate* them.' Nothing less than annihilation.

In somewhat broader terms, Nelson's Mediterranean fleet had to blockade the French fleet in Toulon, and later the Spanish fleet in its bases. If either should escape, they must be prevented from combining forces with the other, and suffer destruction.

Bonaparte appointed Admiral Louis Latouche-Tréville, who had driven off Nelson's attack on Boulogne, as Commander of the Toulon squadron. He was succeeded in November 1804 by Pierre Villeneuve, an officer who had had the good sense and good fortune

A photograph showing Nelson's flagship, the *Victory*, at Portsmouth where she lies today.

144

to escape from the holocaust of Aboukir Bay in his flagship *Guillaume Tell*. The grand design of Bonaparte, who was created Emperor Napoleon in 1805, was to bring about the naval union with his ally, the combined fleet ravaging British trade and possessions in the West Indies, from which so much British wealth derived. Then, their task completed, they would head east again towards a demoralized England, smashing the Royal Navy off Ushant – for long the pivotal point of Britain's maritime defence – and up the Channel to cover the long-planned invasion by the Grand Army, now 150,000 strong. To a military commander, who had experienced few setbacks in his land campaigns, this plan appeared tidy and simple to accomplish.

Impatient as Nelson was by temperament, no one understood better the need for patience and constant alertness in watching an enemy. From his base in Sardinia, where his ships could rest and water and revictual in rotation, Nelson organized an observing blockade intended to hive out the French fleet rather than lock it into its Toulon base. He wanted it well out to sea, too far for crippled units to limp back after the smashing defeat he would inflict upon them.

For weary months, Nelson's frigates rolled and pitched or endured the heat of summer calms, always observing the French mastheads inside Toulon harbour, their signal halyards watched with equal care from the distant big ships.

But the French commander knew they were there, these great ships of the line that had smashed the French fleet, and the Emperor's Eastern campaign, only a few years earlier. And the knowledge of their relentless proximity was unnerving for a fleet whose morale and self-confidence were not high.

As so often before, the only certain French ally was the weather, and when at last this turned foul in January 1805, the French fleet broke free from its bonds, unseen by its observers in a north-westerly gale. Following his instinct, and his belated luck of '98, Nelson made for Alexandria again when he received the signal, from his temporarily blinded frigates, that his quarry had escaped. As in June '98, the Egyptian harbour was empty. If Villeneuve had been here, he had left again rapidly; and at Malta, Nelson learned that the French squadron was back in Toulon. It was only the preliminary lap in one of the longest and most critical chases in naval history.

ABOVE A French
cartoon showing
Napoleon's plans for
the invasion of
England.

On 30 March, Villeneuve again escaped from Toulon, broke through the Strait of Gibraltar, and made Cadiz safely. The link-up had been made at last, the first stage of Napoleon's plan was complete, as tidily as the Emperor had expected. The Spanish Admiral, Federico Carlos de Gravina, made sail and followed his French consort clear across the Atlantic, the combined force making a formidable fleet of 20 sail of the line, 8 frigates, and smaller vessels.

Nelson again lamented his ill-luck. 'My good fortune seems flown away. I cannot get a fair wind, or even a side wind. Dead foul!' Unlike Villeneuve, he was locked into the Mediterranean, until 6 May quite ignorant of the combined enemy fleet's whereabouts or destination. On that day he received intelligence that Villeneuve was headed for the Caribbean, and that he had a long start. What should he do now? Pursue him, in the hope of limiting his depredations and bringing him to battle? Or lie in wait for his inevitable return? The chase could be a wild-goose one. Nelson decided to take the risk, and go. It was a risk for some of his ships, too, which were in sad need of a refit after months of work in Mediterranean heavy seas.

FACING PAGE The
French Vice-Admiral
Villeneuve who led
Nelson a merry chase
in the Atlantic until
he finally met defeat
at the Battle of
Trafalgar.

Villeneuve was already at Martinique, with orders to wait thirty-five days, no more no less, for the arrival of Admiral Honoré Ganteaume, who was to take over the command for the final Channel assault that was to lead to the launch of the invasion. If Ganteaume failed to make the rendezvous, Villeneuve was to sail first for Ferrol and then Brest, to release the blockaded ships at these bases – no fewer than 21 at Brest alone. A vast armada, more powerful by far than Spain's in 1588. Then Boulogne.

It sounded, once again, neat and inevitably culminating in victory. The plan took no account of Nelson's fearsome reputation, and its impact upon the French admiral. Within three days of the receipt of the Emperor's orders, news like a death knell that Nelson was heading west across the Atlantic reached Villeneuve at Martinique. For four days, the admiral fought a losing battle against his own fear. On 8 June 1805, he quit his station and hastened back to Europe.

Villeneuve had little reason for fear, little reason for this precipitate departure. For Nelson was pursued by ill-luck as tenaciously as he was pursuing his antagonist. Misled by innocently false as well as deliberately false intelligence, his weary fleet dodged about the islands of the West Indies in search of the French fleet. It was as puzzling and tantalizing as that summer chase in the eastern Mediterranean. Extracts from his Journal reflect his exasperation: 'very miserable, which is very foolish'; 'It appears hard but as it pleases God, he knows what is best for us poor weak mortals'; 'No French Fleet, nor any information about them. How sorrowful this makes me, but I cannot help myself'.

By 20 July he was back at Gibraltar, and went ashore. He had been continuously on duty in his flagship for two years. Later, he learned that Admiral Sir Robert Calder, the officer who had counted the growing enemy fleet to his admiral at the Cape St Vincent engagement, had intercepted Villeneuve. He had cut off and seized two of the Spanish ships, but had allowed the remainder to escape in poor visibility. At any other time, before Nelson established a new definition of the word, he might have been honoured for a victory, if only a partial one.

For Nelson, looking back over these past two years, he, too, felt that he had failed his country. The truth, expressed by Sir William Hamilton's successor as British Ambassador at Naples, Hugh Elliot (Lord Minto), later reassured him. Recalling the vast

distances sailed by Nelson's fleet, Elliot wrote that 'to have kept your ships afloat, your rigging standing, and your crews in health and spirits is an effort such as never was realized in former times, nor, I doubt, will ever again be repeated by any other admiral. You have protected us for two long years, and you saved the West Indies by only a few days.'

On 18 August 1805 the *Victory* was working her way up to Spithead, and Nelson was gazing upon English fields and woodlands and downs again. What sort of a welcome could he expect, returning home this time without any great victory to his name?

He descended to his barge, a frail, pale figure in his admiral's uniform, right sleeve as always tucked into his coat, green shade protecting his good eye; and, sitting upright in the stern on the polished mahogany seat, was rowed to the shore. There was a crowd on the quayside. As he approached, he saw that they were waving their hats and he could hear their cheers. He had no need to fear that his reputation had in any way diminished.

After the prolonged formalities of arrival, Nelson ordered a post-chaise and set off in the darkness up the London road the next evening. He drove through the night, and arrived at Merton soon after dawn. It was 20 August 1805. Ahead of him he had twenty-five days of peace and pleasure on land before he embarked for his last, and greatest, and most fateful battle.

There was much work to be done, too, during this brief period ashore. Besides his own affairs and the perennial worries about money, Nelson had to be in London during most days to consult with the new First Lord. The wise and percipient Lord Barham was only one of many illustrious figures in charge of the nation's affairs who wished to see Nelson. The huzza-ing crowds at Portsmouth were only an overture to the chorus in London. Fear was rife in the capital. Only by a hair's breadth had Jamaica been saved from the French. A great convoy bound from India and carrying wealth from the East had not yet arrived. Would it do so? Might not Villeneuve emerge to gobble it up? Had not this same French admiral escaped with ease, and with so little loss, from Sir Robert Calder, as he had escaped from Nelson at Aboukir Bay?

Fear and confusion were what Nelson found in London. And he also discovered that he, as never before, was looked up to as the only sure shield, the only saviour, of the nation and its wealth. He had thought he had failed, and now the country, having cheered itself hoarse, was on its knees for his services. His 'wild-goose chase', as he saw it, to the West Indies, when he had complained of his continuing bad luck, was seen in the City, and by the public, as a finely timed masterstroke. Then Calder's failure – and how they were baying for his blood! – had served only to brighten his own star, the victor of the Battles of Cape St Vincent, of Aboukir Bay, of Copenhagen and a dozen more battles.

On that first day in London, his engagements had included visits to the Navy Agents, the Navy Office, the Admiralty, a firm of silver-smiths to order engraved cutlery for little Horatia, then on to the Prime Minister's office, where William Pitt made amply clear to him that his services would again be wanted, and imminently, too.

On fourteen of the twenty-five days left to him before he sailed, he was in London. Nor was there much peace at Merton, where 'Paradise' had become a confusion of crowds – of friends and relations and friends of relations *and* their children. On Sunday, the whole Merton entourage proceeded to church, and filled it to bursting point. Everyone with the remotest connections with the family

A chance meeting between Nelson and the future Duke of Wellington took place at the Colonial Office on 13 September 1805.

FACING PAGE Horatia Nelson.
INSET A letter sent from Nelson to Horatia from the *Victory* on 20 January 1804.

Victory Jan: 20: 1804

My Dear Horatia

I send You a Watch
which I give You permission to Wear
on Sundays, and on very particular
days when you are Dresed and have
behaved exceedingly Well and Obedient
I have kissed it and send it with the
affectionate Blessing of Your
Nelson & Bronte

Victory Jan: 20: 1804

wanted to see the hero. Lord Minto called one day 'and found Nelson just sitting down to dinner, surrounded by a family party, of his brother, the Dean, Mrs Nelson, their children, and the children of a sister, Lady Hamilton at the head of the table and Mother Cadogan at the bottom.'

'We have room for you all,' was the clarion cry of Lady Hamilton, whose gregarious, loving heart was as full as the house. 'So come as soon as you can. We shall be happy, most happy. Here are Sir Peter Parker, and God knows who, so Nelson has not time to say more than that he loves you, and shall rejoice to see you.'

They found it just as Emma described. They found, too, the house much altered. In Nelson's absence, she had carried out many expensive conversions, and had even arranged for a broad brick tunnel to be built beneath the road to save the inconvenience of crossing it from the stable yard. The lady of the house had also ordered a walk to be built for her admiral – an admiral's walk to simulate his own quarterdeck, leading to a new summer house which she laughingly christened 'the Poop'.

Nelson, while wondering anxiously how he was ever going to pay all the bills, paced his quarterdeck and divulged his tactics in the inevitable culminating battle with the combined French and Spanish fleets. It was September, and the days were closing in, and the fleets, when they met, would be great in numbers. 'No day can be long enough to arrange a couple of Fleets,' he told his old friend, Captain Richard Keats, 'and fight a decisive Battle, according to the old system. When *we* meet them, (for meet them we shall), I'll tell you how I shall fight them.'

Somehow, amid the social hurly-burly of Merton and the anxious political and economic tumult of London, Nelson found time for reflection as well as plans. The fear in the City was shared about equally for the combined enemy fleet's renewed attack on the West Indies and the sweep up the Channel to cover the invasion by the Grand Army. One nightmare was as great as the other.

Nelson had reached a different conclusion, which he divulged to his brother-in-law, George Matcham, adding that he must leave at once (it was Saturday evening, 31 August) to tell the Prime Minister. The enemy, when combined, would make for Toulon or Cadiz. 'They will then have collected sixty or seventy sail-of-the-line, and then there will be a difficulty in overcoming them.'

A gold drinking cup ordered by Nelson for Horatia shortly before he left England for the last time.

Nelson's second-in-command at Trafalgar was Vice-Admiral Collingwood.

Adverse odds were like a provocative scent, drawing him to battle. But seventy of the enemy, against perhaps twenty or twenty-five that he could muster? There might, as he thought, indeed be 'a difficulty'.

Nelson saw Pitt again on Sunday. The Prime Minister had recently presided over a Cabinet meeting, which had reached the conclusion that the West Indies would be the combined fleet's destination, and counter-measures should be taken accordingly. After a few minutes with Nelson, his mind was changed. They must, moreover, act at once.

And who was to be the Commander-in-Chief?

Nelson: You cannot have a better man than the present one – Collingwood.

Pitt: No. That won't do. You must take the command.

Nelson objected again, knowing the answer.

Pitt: Will you be ready to sail in three days?

Nelson: I am ready now.

Nelson returned to Merton that Sunday evening. At five o'clock the following morning, a post-chaise raced up the gravel drive. The passenger was Captain Henry Blackwood, one of Nelson's closest friends, the most brilliant of all frigate captains. He had dispatches from Collingwood for Lord Barham and had decided that, being on the road, Nelson should have the news first.

Nelson, ever the early riser, was fully dressed and met him at the door. When he learned that Blackwood had just arrived he said, 'I am sure that you bring me news of the French and Spanish Fleets, and that I shall have to beat them yet.'

Blackwood nodded. They were combined, at Cadiz, as Nelson had predicted. 'I hope that I shall be present at the drubbing, Sir.'

Blackwood proceeded on his way, while Nelson prepared to follow him. He went to Emma's room, awoke her, and told her of the visit, and what it meant. She took it well. This was Emma at her best: stoical, courageous even, accepting the inevitable, determined to conceal her alarm, ready with every support for him – her husband as she now regarded him.

Nelson responded as she would have wished. 'Brave Emma! good Emma! If there were more Emmas there would be more Nelsons.'

The last night at Merton, the house suddenly quiet and empty as if for a funeral with few mourners. Nelson on his knees at Horatia's bedside, praying that she might be happy. A final farewell to Emma.

Friday Night at half-past Ten [wrote Nelson in his Journal] drove from dear, dear Merton, where I left all which I hold dear in this World, to go to serve my King and Country. May the Great God Whom I adore enable me to fulfill the expectations of my Country, and if it is His good pleasure that I should return, my thanks will never cease being offered up to the Throne of His Mercy. If it is His good providence to cut short my days upon Earth, I bow with the greatest submission, relying that He will protect those so dear to me that I may leave behind. His Will be done. Amen, Amen, Amen.

Nelson's departure from England was as moving an experience as his arrival off Cadiz to take over the command from Collingwood. Of the crowds at Portsmouth, Nelson had commented to his flag-captain Hardy, 'I had their huzzas before. I have their hearts now.' On board the *Victory*, on 28 September 1805, he wrote, 'The reception I met on joining the Fleet caused the sweetest sensation of my life.'

Collingwood had always commanded with 'a taut hand', and was without a sense of humour. A big, burly, steady and dutiful officer, he had none of Nelson's style or zest. The whole Fleet was in need of the human touch, the Nelson touch, in more ways than one, and 'the officers who came on board to welcome my return forgot my rank as Commander-in-Chief in the enthusiasm with which they greeted me.'

On the following day, fifteen of these captains dined with Nelson in his great cabin and toasted his forty-seventh birthday. Nelson replied by divulging the plan he had devised in England. The scene has been depicted by artists: Nelson at the cleared table, a chart before him, charged or empty glasses, standing or sitting officers all attention, all silent, as Nelson begins to speak.

The gist of what he told them followed what he had described to Keats back at Merton:

I shall form the Fleet into three Divisions in three Lines. One Division shall be composed of twelve or fourteen of the fastest two-decked Ships, which I shall always keep to windward, or in a situation of advantage; and I shall put them under an Officer who, I am sure, will employ them in the manner I wish, if possible. I consider it will always be in my power to throw into Battle at any part I may choose; but if circumstances prevent their being carried against the Enemy where I desire, I shall feel certain he will employ them effectually, and, perhaps, in a more advantageous manner than if he could have followed my orders.

With the remaining part of the Fleet formed in two Lines, I shall go

A detail from *Farewell to Nelson* by Andrew Gow, showing Nelson's departure from Portsmouth.

to them at once, if I can, about one-third of their Line from their leading Ship . . . I think it will surprise and confound the Enemy. They won't know what I am about. It will bring forward a pell-mell Battle, and that is what I want.

'When I came to explain to them the "*Nelson touch*", it was like an electric shock. Some shed tears, all approved – "It was new – it was singular – it was simple!" and, from admirals downwards it was repeated – "It must succeed . . ."'

A 'pell-mell battle', the British ships laid close alongside the enemy, with the twin ingredients of victory, the superior will and certainty of superiority, and superior gunnery. The risks of breaking with tradition, and breaking the enemy line with twin simultaneous line-ahead attacks at right angles were grave indeed. During the run in, the leading British ships would be subjected to the full broadsides of as many as half a dozen of the enemy, with no opportunity to return the fire. They would inevitably take a battering, but Nelson judged shrewdly that the damage would not prove fatal. He had the widest experience of French gunnery, both of its speed and accuracy, and he believed the vanguard would survive,

BELOW LEFT A plan showing the position of the English, French and Spanish fleets at the beginning of the Battle of Trafalgar. BELOW RIGHT Nelson explaining his plan of attack to his officers.

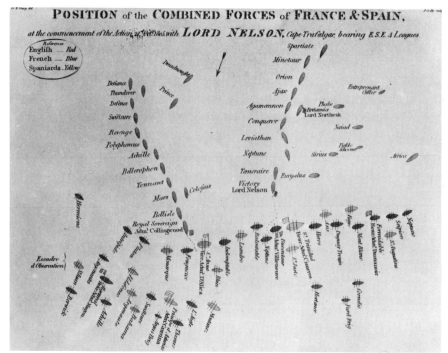

especially if opposed by Spaniards, of whom he rightly held an even lower opinion.

But the advantages were not only of surprise. Theoretically, none of the enemy would be able to slip away; in half the time, *all* would be engaged and victory could come the sooner, within the day.

Now the tight blockade Collingwood had been applying, as if corking up the enemy pending the arrival of the epicure, was relaxed, and Nelson took his big ships out of sight of Cadiz, in the hope of tempting Villeneuve to make a run for Cartagena or Toulon through the Strait of Gibraltar. Only the 'eyes of the Fleet', the frigates, under Henry Blackwood, would continue to keep a watch upon the masts of the combined Franco-Spanish fleet.

Nelson believed that his fleet would not have to face another long, wearying winter of blockade. While Villeneuve remained in port, his 22,000-odd men had to be provisioned, and food in the city was known to be short. Meanwhile, the training of the British fleet continued, consultations and conferences were held daily, all prepared for battle. Reinforcements arrived. One of these was especially welcome: the *Agamemnon*, with dear old Berry in command. Nelson's stump wagged like a pleased dog's tail when the big ship hove into sight: 'Here comes that damned fool Berry!' he exclaimed. '*Now* we shall have a battle.'

Sir Robert Calder was to be court-martialled for his earlier failure and was ordered home, in a frigate, the Admiralty specified. Nelson could not bear this indignity for his fellow admiral and insisted that he should have a ship of the line for the passage, however precious was each one. 'He is in adversity, and if he has ever been my enemy, he now feels the pang of it, and finds me one of his best friends.' What was the loss of a ship? It was the Nelson touch again, and the Fleet gloried in the gesture.

On 2 October, Nelson deprived himself of five more ships, which required water and provisions, and were needed to escort an important convoy through the Strait.

Villeneuve learned of the departure of this powerful force some days later. The intelligence forced his hand. By 18 October, there were two other factors that favoured making the break: the wind had backed to the south, which was advantageous to him and disadvantageous to any pursuing foe; and he had received a fateful message from Madrid. This message had informed him that he was to be superseded as Commander-in-Chief, and that his successor had already arrived in the city. The imminent shame was too much for a proud man. He would escape, or fight it out.

Blackwood's eyes observed the signs, the unmistakable signs – topsails set – of a great fleet stirring. Signals fluttered at the halyards, and were passed on.

> My dearest beloved Emma, [wrote Nelson that night] the dear friend of my bosom, the signal has been made that the Enemy's combined fleet are coming out of Port. We have very little wind, so that I have no hopes of seeing them before tomorrow. May the God of Battles crown my endeavours with success. At all events I will take care that my name shall ever be most dear to you and Horatia, both of whom I love as much as my own life; and as my last writing before the battle will be to you, so I hope in God that I shall live to finish my letter after the Battle. May heaven bless you, prays your *Nelson and Brontë.*

Nelson's favourite portrait of Emma, wearing the Maltese cross, was painted in Dresden in 1800 by J. Schmidt; the painting hung in Nelson's cabin on the *Victory.*

The alarm was no false one, as some had feared. For a while, the possibility had to be considered that the Franco-Spanish force would put back into port as soon as Nelson's great ships were sighted. By the morning of 21 October (the anniversary, Nelson remembered with satisfaction, of Uncle Maurice Suckling's great fight), with the wind veering again to the west, there could be no doubt that battle would be joined that day.

The preliminaries to Trafalgar were played out in the stately, measured pace of all great battles in the age of sail. The wind remained light in the morning, and there was little for anyone to do on either side except (for those who could) to write last letters home, chalk messages of defiance on the barrels of the guns, play games and reminisce. There was a bright sun after the clearance of early morning haze, and it was warm and close on the gun decks, with only a light breeze from abaft the port beam blowing them along no faster than a man can swim. From time to time a ship's band struck up, often several together, playing 'Rule Britannia' or 'Britons Strike Home', adding a festive note, as if this mass of great stubby vessels with all sails set were departing in celebratory triumph from their scene of battle instead of heading, as yet unharmed, towards it. The men danced the hornpipe to the jollier airs, and sang, mainly loudly and tunelessly.

The combined enemy fleet of 18 French and 15 Spanish ships of the line (including the 136-gun *Santissima Trinidad* and scarcely smaller *Santa Ana*) had been in sight since dawn, silhouetted

FACING PAGE Nelson in his cabin before the battle.
INSET Nelson wrote his last letter to Emma on the eve of the Battle of Trafalgar.

Victory Oct: 19: 1805
Noon Cady 2SE 16 Leagues

My Dearest beloved Emma the dear
friend of my bosom the Signal has
been made that the Enemys combined
fleet are coming out of Port, We
have very little Wind so that I have
no hopes of seeing them before tomorrow
May the God of Battles crown my
Endeavours with success at all events
I will take care that my name shall ever
be most dear to you and Horatia both
of whom I love as much as my own
life, and as my last writing before the

against the early light. They made a formidable impression, especially by contrast with the 23 which was all Nelson had been able to muster. But scarcely a single British sailor was dismayed by the odds. On the contrary, odds in their own favour would have been viewed as an affront, as a reflection on their fighting prowess, and (most important of all) as a risk to the total of each man's prize money.

So, the enemy's apparent absence of formation, and their slow turn through 16 points – 180 degrees – was noted with scathing comments by many sailors. They were running for it! Just like the Frogs and Dons! And they couldn't keep station to save their lives!

The Franco-Spanish fleet did seem to be in a state of shambles, even before the turn. But more discerning observers recognized that it was too late for Villeneuve to secure himself back in Cadiz, with the veering of the wind to the west. They judged that he was attempting to consolidate his scattered force, fearful of suffering piecemeal losses from isolated units.

They were right. He had already written a tactical statement for the use of his Staff: Nelson would try to double the rear of the combined fleets, 'cut through our line, and bring against the ships thus isolated groups of his own, to surround and capture them.' And, in an effort to rally the spirits of his pessimistic commanders, Villeneuve had added, 'Captains must rely upon their courage and love of glory' to bring about a successful conclusion.

Every man in both fleets (some 35,000 in all) had several hours to contemplate the battle that must be joined by midday. They might believe that the outcome was inevitable or uncertain, but very few of them failed to consider the possibility of their own death, or injury.

Nelson was one of the few officers who did not enjoy a single idle moment from long before dawn. He was on the quarterdeck at first light, wearing his usual very worn undress uniform coat, the skirts lined not with silk, like most senior officers, but with shalloon. As usual before combat, his manner and speech were animated, his conversation rapid, precise and wide-ranging in subject. He talked in turn to many officers, including the frigate captains who had been summoned on board. He was the complete professional at the height of his powers, like some great conductor before a taxing symphony.

At twenty to seven Nelson had ordered the signal to form two columns. Ten minutes later it was 'Bear up and sail large on the course given', that course being east-north-east. And later still, signal Number 13, 'Prepare for battle'.

Blackwood and Hardy were asked to come below to witness his signature to what he called 'my last Codicil'. The refusal of the King and many prominent people in Society and power to accept Emma had hurt Nelson bitterly. In the event of his death, he had no cause to fear for his wife or family, who were well provided for with trusts and grants. He had every reason to fear for the welfare and security of Emma Hamilton, and he had drawn up an elaborate appeal to his country on her behalf, beginning, 'Whereas the eminent services of Emma Hamilton . . . have been of the very greatest service to our King and Country.' And ending, 'Could I have rewarded these services, I would not now call upon my Country; but as this has not been in my power,' he continued, 'I leave Emma Lady Hamilton, therefore, a Legacy to my King and Country, that they will give her an ample provision to maintain her rank in life.' There was a similar appeal on behalf of Horatia. 'These are the only favours I ask of my King and Country at this moment when I am going to fight their battle.' Signed and witnessed 'Nelson and Brontë'.

Blackwood, like the ship's surgeon, William Beatty, was con-

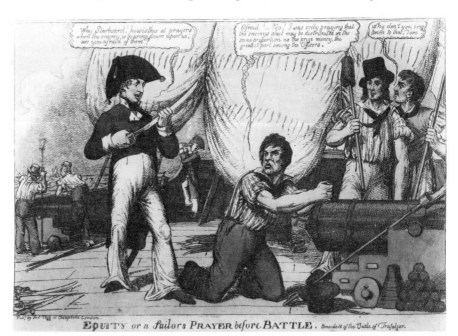

A cartoon contemporary to the Battle of Trafalgar criticizing the low rates of pay for sailors compared to that of the officers who had honours heaped upon them as well as gaining large sums of prize money.

cerned about the safety of his Commander-in-Chief, and now suggested that he should shift his flag, because the *Victory* was well known as his ship and would be the target for every enemy gunner, especially of the sharpshooters who would certainly be packed in the rigging. Nelson brushed the suggestion aside. What a poor example it would make to the men if their leader seemed concerned only for his safety! Later, he agreed to the suggestion that he should change his coat to conceal the orders on his chest, which stood out like shooting-gallery targets; then he said, inaccurately, that there was no time.

Nelson did, however, agree in principle that several more ships should proceed ahead of the *Victory* so that the flagship should at least share the first, and terrible, blows that would inevitably be aimed at her.

He was heard to say, 'Let them go!' But simultaneously, he saw to it that every inch of sail was set, in the hope of increasing his speed by even the smallest margin. And when the *Téméraire* threatened to overtake the *Victory*, Nelson was heard to hail her captain indignantly, 'I'll thank you, Captain Harvey, to keep in your proper station . . .'

Shortly before eleven o'clock Nelson went below after measuring the distance to the enemy, who were now very close. Here he wrote

162

FACING PAGE Nelson, wearing the undress uniform of a vice-admiral, gives the orders to hoist his famous signal at the beginning of the action.
RIGHT The flags flown from the *Victory* sending out Nelson's message to the rest of the British fleet; an engraving from *The Boy's Own Paper* showing also what happened to the *Victory* after the battle.

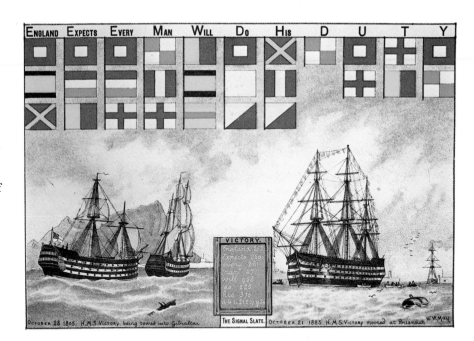

in his private diary, inspired to deep passion and humility by the momentousness of the time and occasion, a last prayer:

> May the Great God whom I worship Grant to my Country and for the benefit of Europe in General a great and Glorious Victory, and may no misconduct in anyone tarnish it, and may humanity after Victory be the predominant feature in the British Fleet. For myself individually I commit my life to Him Who made me, and may His blessing light upon my endeavours for serving my Country faithfully. To Him I resign myself and the just cause which is entrusted me to Defend. Amen, Amen, Amen.

Nelson was observed to be alone and upon his knees at this time by his signal-lieutenant, John Pascoe, who entered to make a personal request regarding promotion, but who slipped out again, embarrassed and unseen.

Back on the quarterdeck, Nelson recognized that the first ranging shots would soon be fired, and that the action must then become general. Turning to Pascoe, he indicated that he wished to 'amuse' the fleet with a special signal, and that it was to read, 'Nelson confides that every man will do his duty.' There was little time left for the hoist, and the lieutenant asked leave for the sake of speed to substitute 'England' for 'Nelson', and 'expects' for 'confides'. Nelson agreed to this; and 'England expects that every man will do

163

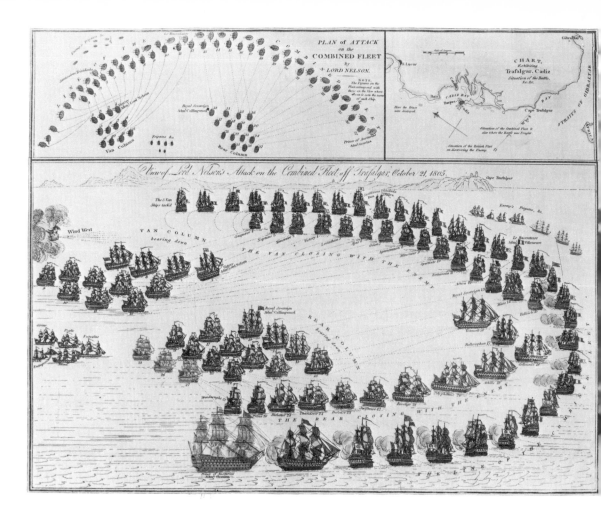

his duty' was the final, historic wording that went out to the fleet.

As usual, Nelson's sense of what would be most personally inspiring was right. In their closed world of professional fighting sailors, the kinship and loyalty to distant England was as nothing compared with their love of their leader; and the word 'expects' was resented by some old-timers as being too mandatory. But they cheered all the same.

Nelson had not received sufficient reinforcements to form the third division specified in his plan, and all his twenty-three ships of the line were incorporated in the two divisions still on their east-north-easterly heading. They were like two spears aimed at the four-mile-long enemy line, which was drawn up like a concave shield protecting the Spanish mainland. But it was no tidy pattern measured out here ten miles off the coast. For most of its length the

A plan of the Battle of Trafalgar published in November 1805 showing the British fleet advancing upon the combined forces of the French and Spanish fleets.

164

line was no line at all, with as many as three big ships abreast of one another. Except for the *Africa*, which had missed a signal and was still some eight miles to the west, the British 'spears' remained as more or less straight lines, but the distance between the ships varied according to their sailing qualities.

Half-past eleven. It was clear that Collingwood's eastern division would strike the Franco-Spanish fleet first. The *Royal Sovereign* had recently been recoppered and was an especially fast sailer. Collingwood's flagship, then, would suffer the first shots, then *Belleisle*, and *Mars*, *Colossus* and *Tonnant*, *Bellerophon* and *Achilles*, *Polyphemus* and *Revenge*: the names like a roll call of British maritime warfare.

Ten minutes later, the mellow sounds of the water swishing slowly along the wooden hulls, the mutter of voices, the occasional shout or burst of laughter, the perky melodies from the ships' bands – all these friendly sounds were overwhelmed by a crashing broadside that broke the long suspense and pent-up tension, and a puff of grey smoke arose from the French *Fougeaux*, 74, in the dead centre of the enemy line. The range was one thousand yards, and her target was, inevitably, the *Royal Sovereign*, which would be alone against this formidable line of ships for many minutes, and unable to answer. It was a nerve-testing ordeal, and Collingwood ordered his men to lie down as a second and third broadside tore into his ship. He was bringing her between the Spanish *Santa Ana*,

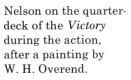

Nelson on the quarter-deck of the *Victory* during the action, after a painting by W. H. Overend.

112, and French *Indomptable*, 80, and already she was half-concealed in smoke, her sails in tatters, much of her rigging gone, a number of her men killed or wounded. Then, as she passed under the unprotected stern of the *Santa Ana*, flying the flag of Vice-Admiral de Álava, the British gunners were able to exact their own payment for the drubbing they had received: a full 50-gun double-shotted ripple broadside at 30 yards' range that tore into the Spanish flagship with devastating effect. A minute later, in a third of the time the enemy could reload, the *Royal Sovereign* fired her port guns again.

Nelson had earlier been watching his old friend's ship being smashed by the guns of no fewer than five of the enemy. 'See how that noble fellow Collingwood carries his ship into action,' he said to those about him.

Then, a few seconds later, watching keenly the engagement that had opened on the *Victory*'s starboard bow with the *Royal Sovereign* now locked in desperate embrace with the *Santa Ana*, he heard Pascoe exclaim, 'There is a topgallant yard gone!'

Nelson asked 'Whose? Is it the *Royal Sovereign*'s?' And when he was reassured, added, 'Collingwood is doing well.'

Nelson's flag was clearly seen by the ships in the van of the enemy line before the smoke blanketed the identity of all but the nearest vessels. The temptation to put a ball into her was too great to resist, and several distant French and Spanish vessels tried ranging shots. The *Santissima Trinidad*, *Bucentaure* and *Héros* fired at the British flagship as she sailed on towards them, all sails set, gun ports open and guns run out, as bright in her new paint as she appeared indestructible: the same three-decker which had battered the Spaniards at Cape St Vincent 200 miles to the west eight years earlier, and now flying the flag of the admiral who had annihilated the French at the other end of the Mediterranean seven years ago.

At the *Victory*'s halyards flew Nelson's final signal. Inevitably, it ran, 'Engage the enemy more closely.'

Blackwood, his wish 'to be present at the drubbing' soon to be fulfilled, had embarked in a boat for his frigate a few minutes before it was hoisted, Nelson's last words ringing in his ears:

'Now I can do no more. We must trust to the great disposer of all events.' Then, as Blackwood made for the gangway, 'God bless you, Blackwood. I shall not speak to you again.'

Though the men knew what was coming, though the officers

RIGHT The Battle of Trafalgar as seen from the mizzen shrouds of the *Victory*, painted by J. M. W. Turner.

BELOW The *Victory*, painted by Turner who went to visit the ship at Sheerness when she was brought back to England a month after the battle.

knew, and were perhaps reassured, that it was called the Nelson touch, the waiting had been almost unendurable, even for the hardiest veteran behind the guns or on deck. Several of those first ranging balls fell in the water, sending up white spouts. Then one tore through the main topgallant sail.

The French crews who observed this trivial damage sent up a cheer that rose above the sound of gunfire. Another shot, almost simultaneous, more merited a cheer. The ball passed close by Hardy, cutting Nelson's secretary almost in two. His remains were cast overboard speedily by some marines. But Nelson was not to be deceived. 'Is that poor Scott who is gone?' he was heard to say. 'Poor fellow!'

Now that the range was established, at least half a dozen of the enemy had begun to fire full broadsides, not all accurately in the rising swell, but enough seriously to damage the flagship, which, like the *Royal Sovereign* ten minutes earlier, could only suffer defencelessly. After a number of vulnerable marines had been killed, Nelson ordered them to scatter about the ship, and almost everyone except himself and Hardy and his staff were taking cover from the concentration of fire from the *Héros*, *Bucentaure*, *Santissima Trinidad* and others.

In a moment the *Victory*'s mizzen topmast was down, trailing rigging across the deck, and all her studding sails were shot away. A single ball tore across the quarterdeck close to Nelson, cut the tiller ropes and smashed the wheel. Another ball struck the deck ahead of Hardy and Nelson as they paced up and down. It ricocheted between them like a sudden blast of wind, and a splinter of wood tore off the buckle of Hardy's shoe.

This at last caused the two officers to halt in their tracks, and exchange looks. Nelson smiled, for the last time, that confiding, warm smile on his full lips that had beguiled so many men and women. 'This is too warm work, Hardy, to last for long.' He recommenced walking, remarking that he had never seen such cool courage as the *Victory*'s crew were demonstrating that day.

One by one the other ships of the van in both columns were becoming involved: *Téméraire*, *Neptune*, *Britannia*, *Leviathan*, *Bellerophon*, *Achilles*, *Polyphemus*. The later ships overtook those disabled by the crushing fire of the massed enemy, the gun crews and marines cheering one another on before the smoke of battle obscured the comforting sight of fellow countrymen at their guns.

Amid the choking smoke, the chaos, the confusion and suffering and blood, the thunderous noise that would deafen so many for life – from all this no pattern emerged. No pattern, but an implacable trend, an imbalance of success over failure regardless of weight of shot, of number of cannon and carronades, muskets and grenades, slowly shaped itself out of the chorus of screams and detonations, and the criss-cross web of collapsed yards and spars, masts and rigging; in the water, the swimming, the drowning, and the dead. After those first enemy ranging shots Hardy had expressed his concern about their precise course. He knew, as everyone now knew, that the enemy line was to be pierced; and the price they would have to pay had (in mathematical terms) been accounted for. But just where – between the *Douquay Trouin* and *Héros*? the *Héros* and *Santissima Trinidad*? – in this curved, confused enemy line it was hard to select your own first adversaries when there were so many. It certainly appeared inevitable that they would strike one of them.

Hardy: It seems impossible, Sir, to cross through the enemy's line without going on board one of their ships.

Nelson: I cannot help it. It does not signify which one we run on board of. Go on board which you please. Take your choice.

Hardy's decision was critical to the shape of the battle, and the fate of his admiral. 'Port the helm!' he shouted to the ship's master, who transmitted the order to the tiller flat, where those forty men were steering the *Victory*.

Slowly, implacably, the helm of the great, half-crippled ship went over, and her bowsprit and bluff stem conformed, pointing head-on at the *Redoutable*, 74, with the *Bucentaure*, 80, next in line on the port beam, and so close that when the *Victory* brushed past, their rigging touched and men could have swung from ship to ship. It had worked out as he had wished at Merton, 'about one third of their line from their leading ship'.

But Hardy could not have selected two more formidable ships for such close engagement. The *Bucentaure* was Villeneuve's flagship; the *Redoutable* well-named as the ship of Captain Jean-Jacques Lucas, the most fearless and determined antagonist in the Allied fleet. At first everything went against the British flagship. Then,

like a copybook repetition of Collingwood's dreadful broadside, as she slipped behind the *Bucentaure*'s elaborately carved and gilded stern, the *Victory*'s port carronades blasted out a devastating volley of 68-pound balls, each accompanied by a keg of 500 musket balls.

The *Bucentaure*'s stern was blown in, as if a hurricane had cast her against a granite cliff. As many as a third of her company were killed or disabled. A double-shotted broadside followed almost at once, and then the *Victory* drifted away slowly, still clutched by Lucas's *Redoutable*, pouring a starboard broadside into her, a port broadside now into the giant *Santissima Trinidad*, who was adding her own unsurpassed firepower to the total that was pounding the *Victory* in return.

Captain Lucas did not believe in gunnery duels, and to the astonishment of the *Victory*'s men had actually closed all his ship's gun ports. Like the Spaniards of old, he believed in the pike and cutlass, supported by such up-to-date weapons as grenades. To Jean-Jacques Lucas, close engagement meant a devastating fire

171

from aloft, an armed party at the ready, grappling irons – then boarding an enemy whose upper decks were now cleared by his sharpshooters.

The one great French hero of the battle, Lucas came surprisingly close to justifying his intentions of capturing both British flagship and Commander-in-Chief.

At twenty five to two, with Nelson and Hardy still pacing the quarterdeck, up and down, up and down, while the musket and grenade fire from Lucas's men was at its most intense and had already killed many on deck, a single sharpshooter identified the figure of the small man, in tricorne hat and with the ornate, glittering orders on his chest, through the smoke rising from below. He took aim, steadied against the roll of both ships, and squeezed the trigger.

The ball struck Nelson on the left shoulder, pierced his chest, and lodged in his spine, with a fragment of epaulette gold braid still adhering to it. A party was desperately attempting to board the *Victory* (several actually succeeded in getting onto her upper deck), before the *Téméraire* closed upon the *Redoutable*'s other quarter and poured in broadside after broadside at point-blank range, like bitter punches of revenge for the injury to their beloved commander. (The French ship suffered some 500 dead, far more than any other ship, and sank the next day.)

As Nelson slipped to the deck, by grotesque coincidence in the blood of his late secretary, Hardy noted his absence at his side almost at once. He turned and saw that Nelson had fallen on his right side, supporting himself momentarily with the finger tips of his only hand. Then he fell forward onto his face.

Few men witnessed the tragedy. All about the admiral men were falling, and the noise and smoke and movement and individual crises of close battle, distracted eyes from the outstretched figure. Hardy ran to him, and bent down, assisting two seamen and a sergeant-major of the Royal Marines.

The ball which mortally wounded Nelson.

Nelson said quite clearly, 'They have done for me at last, Hardy.'

'I hope not, Sir.' He knew well that this was not the first time his admiral had predicted his own death. But things looked bad for him.

'Yes, my backbone is shot through.'

Three seamen carried Nelson off the quarterdeck and down below decks, almost dropping him in their grief and anxiety. Here the din was suddenly subdued and the light dimmed.

A contemporary drawing of Nelson being wounded on the quarter-deck of the *Victory*.

On the middle deck, Nelson's single sailor's eye saw that something was amiss, and he gave orders to Hardy to see that the tiller ropes should be re-rove.

It was a dark, secret world of pain and blood down in the cockpit. Guttering candles and lanterns revealed wounded men on lengths of sailcloth awaiting the attention of the surgeon, some forty in all when Nelson was placed in a nearby midshipman's berth.

Beatty's attention was drawn to Nelson's presence. The admiral

was not readily identifiable as he had insisted on having a handkerchief placed over his face so that his presence would not be immediately noticed.

'Ah, Mr Beatty,' were Nelson's first words. 'You can do nothing for me. I have but a short time to live. My back is shot through.'

The sound of battle was like summer thunder beyond a mountain range.

They cut off Nelson's clothes and covered him with a sheet. The admiral was clearly in acute pain. 'Doctor, I told you so,' he kept saying. 'Doctor, I am gone.' It was almost like a liturgy of fulfilment. And it was followed by a sacrament for his Emma and Horatia. In a soft voice: 'I have to leave Lady Hamilton and my adopted daughter Horatia, as a legacy to my country.' It might be a forlorn prayer, but as a man of faith, it had to be made.

His mind continued active and curious as his life ebbed away. How was the battle going? How was his injury? As always, he was deeply interested in the condition of his own body. 'I felt it break my back.' Beatty examined the wound and asked the patient many questions, which he readily answered: gushes of blood in his breast,

When the House of Lords was rebuilt in the 1840s, frescoes were painted on many of the inner walls, illustrating great moments of British history; this one, over 45 feet long, is in the Royal Gallery and shows the death of Nelson as romanticized by the early Victorians.

difficult breathing, intense pain in the lower part of his spine, no
feeling in the lower part of his body.

Yes, the wound was mortal, Beatty recognized. But the news
must be kept from all but the officers closest about him.

The 32-pounders on the deck above continued to roar out, and
between broadsides, Nelson heard men cheering.

'What is the cause of the cheering? Bring me Hardy? Where is
Hardy?'

Then, when he failed to appear, Nelson became convinced that
he was dead.

'Will no one bring Hardy to me? He must be killed. He is surely
destroyed.'

The word, when it came, was formal and only slightly reassuring.
A midshipman, Bulkeley by name, and only distantly known to
Nelson, put his mouth to the admiral's ear and said, 'Circumstances
respecting the fleet require Captain Hardy's presence on deck, Sir,
but he will avail himself of the first favourable moment to visit his
Lordship.'

'Who is this – who is this?' Nelson demanded of Beatty.

A Staffordshire group commemorating Nelson's death.

'It is Mr Bulkeley, my Lord.'

There was another pause. And then, at this terrible hour, in this awful pain, Nelson's abiding concern for the young and promising still could not be dimmed. 'Yes, it is his voice,' he confirmed to Beatty; and turned his head slightly towards the dimly seen boy. 'Remember me to your father,' he said.

Burly, reassuring, successful in concealing his anxiety and helped in doing so by the dimness of the light down there, Hardy returned to his admiral's side an hour after he had been hit.

He shook his hand and knelt down beside Nelson, who asked, 'Well, Hardy, how goes the battle? How goes the day with us?'

'Very well, my Lord. We have got twelve or fourteen of the enemy's ships in our possession, but five of their van have tacked, and show an intention of bearing down on the *Victory*.' The *Fougeaux* and *Redoutable* had been beaten into silence, but there were still unengaged enemy ships to add to the flagship's suffering.

Hardy continued: 'I have, therefore, called two or three of our fresh ships round us, and have no doubt of giving them a drubbing.'

Nelson was past all healing balm, but the words gave him

176

comfort. Then he asked anxiously, 'I hope none of *our* ships have struck, Hardy?'

'No, my Lord. There is no fear of that.'

'I am a dead man, Hardy. I am going fast. It will be all over with me soon. Come nearer to me . . .'

He wished to speak of Emma. 'Pray let my dear Lady Hamilton have my hair,' he said softly. 'And all other things belonging to me.'

Hardy asked after his pain. 'Is it great, my Lord?'

'Yes, but I shall live half an hour longer yet.'

The faces about him seemed forever to be changing. Hardy's had gone. Now Beatty's was there. 'Look after the others,' Nelson begged him. 'You can do nothing for me. The pain is so severe that I wish I were dead.' His servants were answering his frequent call, 'Rub, rub! Drink, drink!'

Then, pathetically, 'Yet, one would like to live a little longer too.' A pause. 'God be praised, I have done my duty.'

Beatty had been amputating a midshipman's leg, and he now returned to his duties, which were onerous. But a few minutes later, he was recalled to Nelson's bedside.

'Ah, Mr Beatty, I have sent for you to say, what I forgot to tell you before – that all my power of motion and feeling below my breast are gone.'

BELOW The breeches and socks worn by Nelson at the time of his death and reverently preserved.

The surgeon, accustomed to the vagaries of wandering minds close to death, said only, 'My Lord, you told me so before.' But he knew what Nelson wished to hear now, and continued softly, 'My Lord, unhappily for our Country, nothing further can be done for you.' He stepped back to hide his face, and heard Nelson's voice saying, 'I know. I feel something rising in my breast which tells me that I am gone.' A pause, a search for strength. 'God be praised, I have done my duty.' His voice was very quiet, but he was able to repeat the words so that those closest to him could hear.

Other scraps, other messages, reached the ears of those clustering about him, their hearts in despair. 'What would become of poor Lady Hamilton if she knew my situation?' 'Rub, rub! Drink, drink!' A servant held his head, the chaplain poured water . . . A prolonged violent concussion as the 32-pounders on the deck above fired a full broadside. The shock to Nelson's tortured body was too much. 'Oh! *Victory, Victory*! How you distract my poor brain!' Then, 'How dear is life to all men!'

There was Hardy again, his hand holding Nelson's left hand gently where it lay above the sheet, and continuing to hold it as he congratulated the hero on a brilliant victory. He could not say how many of the enemy had been seized because of the smoke and uncertainty, but no fewer than fourteen or fifteen.

'That is well,' replied Nelson. 'But I bargained for twenty. Anchor, Hardy, anchor!'

Hardy said quietly, 'I suppose, my Lord, Admiral Collingwood will now take upon himself the direction of affairs.'

This caused a last spark of defiance, and Nelson attempted unsuccessfully to raise himself. 'Not while I live, I hope, Hardy!'

These were the last moments of life, and Nelson and all those present knew it.

Nelson put it into words, almost his last words. 'In a few minutes I will be no more.' His speech was very soft, and Hardy was leaning close to him. 'Don't throw me overboard, Hardy.'

'Oh no, certainly not.'

'Then you know what to do. Take care of my dear Lady Hamilton, Hardy. Take care of poor Lady Hamilton.'

Hardy was on his knees, and when Nelson asked to be kissed, he did so.

'Now I am satisfied. Thank God, I have done my duty.' Hardy raised himself to his feet, and almost at once, seized with grief and compassion, knelt down again and kissed Nelson's forehead.

'Who is that?'

'It is Hardy.'

'God bless you, Hardy.'

A moment later he asked his valet to turn him upon his right side to ease the pain, and, his mind filled with the scene from the quarterdeck, with the enemy scattered or flying British colours, he said very softly, 'I wish I had never left the deck.'

To the chaplain he said, 'I have not been a great sinner, doctor.' Then the appeal once more, a last gesture of protection and defence: '*Remember*', he said, 'that I leave Lady Hamilton and my daughter as a legacy to my country – never forget Horatia.'

Beatty, the best witness to these hours in the cockpit, heard the last words of all, repeated each time more weakly, 'Thank God, I have done my duty.' At half past four, with the British victory complete, Beatty held his wrist and felt no pulse.

Half an hour later, the French 74, *Achilles*, which had fought so

ABOVE Nelson's last moments below deck, painted by Arthur Devis.

RIGHT A silver gilt snuff box, shown open, in the shape of a mask of Nelson's face.

long and had never struck her colours, blew up, terminating the greatest naval battle of all time with a colossal explosion. Far distant towards the sinking sun a few sails could be observed, the scattered remnants of a broken fleet.

Now there was no holding back from the Fleet the news of the loss of their beloved Commander-in-Chief. It spread like a carronade's concussion from that still, dark corner of pain in the *Victory*'s cockpit, throughout the great wrecked three-decker; then to one, and another, and a third, until every sailor in every ship present,

from the dismasted and ruined *Téméraire* to the untouched *Prince* ('she sails like a haystack'), knew that Nelson was dead. The conflict of feeling from elation at the annihilating victory and satisfying expectation of the prize money, to the grief and sense of loss, caused an additional strain on men stunned and weary from the fight.

Many openly sobbed by their cooling guns amid the litter of battle but few of the men had long to contemplate their survival, their gain or their loss. The seas continued to rise in the early evening, and during the night a storm hit the fleets. Neither victor nor vanquished was equipped to meet it, with tattered sails and rigging, and masts and spars not yet cleared from the upper decks, and overcome with weariness themselves. Tow ropes parted, cherished prizes slipped away in the darkness, while in many ships – the *Victory* was among the worst – the struggle for survival against the new enemy was as arduous and desperate as the mêlée of the previous afternoon. Several of the captured Spanish and French ships were scattered and never recovered. Others were swept onto the lee shore. The *Indomptable*, with 500 survivors from the *Bucentaure* on

The storm after the Battle of Trafalgar, which prevented the British fleet from pursuing any surviving enemy ships.

board, was lost, with one thousand French drowned, struggling to reach shelter.

Collingwood, now in command, ordered other ships to be scuttled and burned, amongst them the mighty *Santissima Trinidad*. Thus, although the net loss of ships to the Allies was twenty-two out of the thirty-three engaged by Nelson, only four prizes were at length taken into possession, and men who had fought so hard and deserved so much appeared likely to gain little financially. In fact, Parliament later voted a special award, so that no seaman gained less than £6 10s, and every captain received £3,362.

The *Victory* herself only just made Gibraltar seven days later. Nelson's body was sealed in a lead coffin filled with brandy, and then later laid in the coffin made from the *L'Orient*'s mast, which had stood by him since the Nile victory. An autopsy had revealed that all his organs were in excellent condition, 'more those of a youth than a man'.

The battle had been observed from the Spanish mainland, and more distantly from the coast of North Africa, as a massive cloud of smoke 'that arose like a mound on the horizon' amid the 'sullen thunder that came up from beyond the sea-line'. But those watchers could learn nothing of the outcome, and the extent of the catastrophe to the Allied fleet which had so recently departed from Cadiz was not made known until the first survivor returned.

Collingwood's dispatch, composed during the height of the storm, brought the first news of Trafalgar to England. A schooner, driven by the same high winds that had led to greater losses than the battle itself, reached Falmouth in eight days. The lieutenant drove straight to London, 265 miles in 37 hours, and the news was in the First Lord's hands by one o'clock in the morning, and the King's soon after dawn.

A Trafalgar medal given to those sailors who had served at the Battle.

181

8

Nelson the Hero

Although the strategic and diplomatic consequences of the victory were even greater than those of the Nile, this time there could be none of the unrestrained excitement and celebration of 1798. *The Times* set the mood: 'We know not whether we should mourn or rejoice. The country has gained the most splendid and decisive Victory . . . but *The great and gallant Nelson is no more.*'

The funeral was the most elaborate and splendid in living memory. Nelson had specified St Paul's for burial, Westminster Abbey (he had heard) being built on a bog and liable one day to subside, taking with it his notion of posterity. It was one wish that was complied with, and so extensive was the procession that the end had not left Whitehall when the head reached the cathedral.

Both his last order, to anchor, and his last wish – his most ardent plea and prayer – were ignored. The loss of lives, and the loss of prizes, was the consequence of the first failure. The nation's disregard for Nelson's 'last codicil' was a disgrace, a blot on the honour of those who knew the depth of his feelings for his mistress and daughter, and on a hypocritical nation whose supposed glorification of the hero was later made to seem so hollow. The sanctimonious Reverend William Nelson, who had trimmed his sails to follow the course of his adulterous brother away from Fanny, received a pension of £5,000 per annum in perpetuity with the Earldom and an estate to which the country contributed £99,000. Emma received nothing. Improvident as always, and overcome with grief, her affairs slipped into chaos, and she was later reduced to escaping from her debtors to Calais, where she died in 1815, at her side Horatia, who lived to be eighty-one.

The Nelson memorial was completed in 1843. Today, what can we make of this man, whose likeness seventeen-feet tall, illuminated at night, faces down Whitehall to the Admiralty, which had once

ABOVE A Nelson mourning ring. FACING PAGE A three-handled jug made by Copelands in 1905 to commemorate the centenary of Nelson's death.

BRITONS!
Your NELSON is dead!
Trust not in an Arm of Flesh, but
in the *Living* GOD!
WHAT SAID THE BRAVE
Nelson, Duncan, Howe?
"GOD hath given us the VICTORY!"
His Arm is not cold in Death, nor
shortened that it cannot Save.
BRITONS!
Fear GOD, Fear SIN, And Then
Fear Nothing.

neglected him for five years and was perforce later persuaded that he was the greatest of all commanders, and that 'There is only one Nelson'? Why did his bargeman Sykes throw himself before that blade to save his life? Why did rough sailors, streaked in sweat and powder dust, cry over their guns for him? Why does the memory of the man nearly 200 years after his victories raise such affection and emotion? Collingwood, too, the admirable, grave, sturdy Collingwood, might have won as great a victory and saved the nation from the threat of invasion and given Britain maritime supremacy for more than a hundred years. Few people besides his wife and some friends would have cried for 'My dear Coll' if he had died the hero's death at the moment of victory. Collingwood was no legend maker, no stylist. He ruled his officers and men in the tradition of aloof distance and harsh discipline.

The hero's gift was of a different order, and was infinite. He was a legend maker and he was very much the stylist. Above all, he

ABOVE Nelson's funeral procession passing under Blackfriars Bridge.
INSET A religious poster published at the time of Nelson's death.

FACING PAGE The order of Nelson's funeral procession from the Admiralty to St Paul's Cathedral.

184

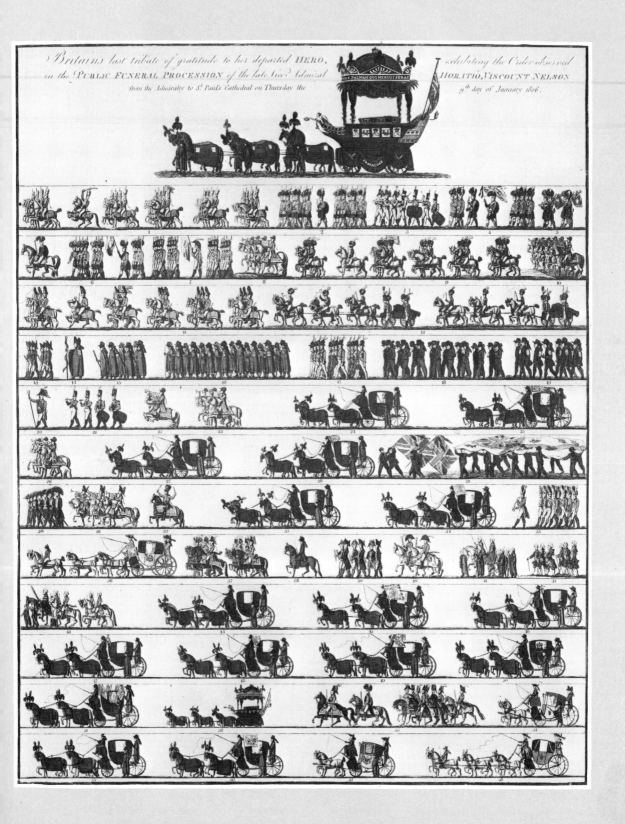

Britains last tribute of gratitude to her departed HERO, exhibiting the Order observed in the PUBLIC FUNERAL PROCESSION of the late Vice-Admiral HORATIO, VISCOUNT NELSON from the Admiralty to S.t Paul's Cathedral on Thursday the 9.th day of January 1806.

A group of snuff boxes commemorating Nelson.

possessed the unique recipe of mystery and passion and, comfortingly, the common touch, so that his contemporaries felt that he was one of them, with all his weaknesses of vanity and of the flesh, and with the physical courage that inspired them to emulate him. They were elevated by his example, and gloried in finding themselves raised to heights of personal valour.

Horatio Nelson was the personification of leadership. His indiscretions and insubordination were as admired as his impulsiveness,

Two papier-mâché boxes depicting the head of Nelson.

186

generosity of spirit, and compassion for the underprivileged and unfortunate. The cruel larger-than-lifeness of the cartoons did no damage to his heroic standing among his men, for they loved the extravagances of their Commander. The higher that the Court and Society raised their eyes to heaven in consternation at his behaviour, the more the Fleet elevated him in their affections.

His love for his fellow sailors remained boundless to the end. When one of his Band of Brothers, Ralph Willett Miller, was killed and a monument proposed, Nelson offered to put up all the money 'for poor dear Miller' if no one else would subscribe. For the inscription, Nelson laid down that 'The language must be plain, as if flowing from the heart of one of us Sailors who have fought with him.' Rank mattered nothing, loyalty and solidarity were all. 'I glory in them, my darling children,' he once wrote of his sailors. 'My brave fellows,' he called them as he stood in line to have his wound at the Nile attended to.

St Vincent and Hood understood this fusion of spirit between Nelson and the men who fought at his side. So did Berry and Miller, Fremantle and Hardy, and the rest. More distant figures sometimes did not begin to comprehend the relationship. Others only half understood, and possessed the humility to admit it. One artist who was commissioned to paint his portrait admitted that he would never be able to commit the secret to canvas. 'There is such a mixture of humanity and ambition in Lord Nelson's countenance,' he confessed, 'that I dare not risk the attempt.'

A late Victorian comic strip telling the life of Nelson.

Horatio Nelson left behind many puzzles and contradictions of character. Certainly the last mystery of his death, the question of whether or not he sought it, can never be satisfactorily resolved.

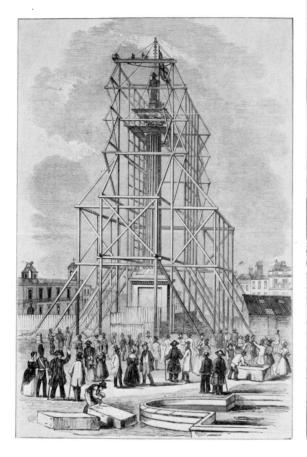

The fact that he paced up and down the quarterdeck after refusing to shift his flag, refusing to allow another ship to take the first crushing effect of the enemy fire, and sidetracking the suggestion that he should conceal his orders, can be used as evidence that he was expecting and even hoping for a hero's death. His personal life, it can be argued, was in as great a state of confusion as his financial affairs. Was the guilt of a good Christian man at his treatment of his wife and his succumbing to the temptations of the flesh too much to bear any longer? With reason, he suspected that he would soon be totally blind.

There is such nobility and neatness as well as tragedy in the hero's end that it is tempting to believe that the rich theatrical element in his character shaped events as they occurred and as they have now formed themselves into the great legend of British history.

This writer does not believe there is any validity in the theories of suicide, or 'semi-suicide'. Nelson had long since reconciled himself

ABOVE LEFT Nelson's column in Trafalgar Square, its progress as seen on 16 November 1843.
ABOVE RIGHT The statue of Nelson at the top of the column.

to his own sins and weaknesses. His love for Emma was immutable and timeless. If he had returned alive, the problems of his social status and financial affairs would have been resolved. An earldom, certainly; a dukedom, perhaps. Even Emma's extravagances would have been absorbed by the wealth an adoring nation would have awarded him.

Nelson paced the quarterdeck of his flagship because that was his duty, to share the dangers his men were facing, like every admiral and captain in the Royal Navy. It was quite beyond consideration that he should cravenly conceal his proud orders. Very little should be read into his predictions of his own death, including that to Blackwood as the battle began. In every fight he knew better than anyone how high were the risks, and was ever the fatalist, as at the Nile with his superficial flesh wound.

What cannot be questioned is that he believed that if the Almighty God decreed that he should die in action, he would do so, and with all the humility and grace and gratitude that he could muster. Perhaps the Lord's judgment might be harsher in retribution for his sins. But no more.

'Thank God I have done my duty,' was not an expression of self-satisfaction. It was an expression of thankfulness to God of a deeply religious man for allowing him to do his duty, and the privilege of setting an example to his beloved nation as the hero.

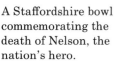

A Staffordshire bowl commemorating the death of Nelson, the nation's hero.

Illustration Acknowledgments

The producers of the book would like to thank the National Maritime Museum at Greenwich and the Royal Naval Museum at Portsmouth for their help with the illustrations.

Anglesey Abbey (National Trust, Photo: John Bethell): 100-1
Barnaby's Picture Library: 124
BBC Hulton Picture Library: 38, 66, 98 (above), 106 (above), 114, 134, 172, 179 (below)
Bibliothèque Nationale, Paris: 75
British Museum: 107 (right)
Museo di Capodimonte, Naples (Photo: Scala): 104
Cooper-Bridgeman Library: 15 (National Maritime Museum), 34 (left) (Collection of the Marquess of Zetland, Richmond, Yorkshire), 117 (Nelson-Macarthy Museum, Portsmouth), 141 (By courtesy of Christies), 145, 169 (above) (The Coram Foundation)
The Daily Telegraph Library: 188 (right)
Department of the Environment (Crown Copyright – reproduced with permission of Her Majesty's Stationery Office): 174-5
John R. Freeman: 21 (above), 62, 76, 86, 93, 125, 130, 167 (above), 188 (left)
Giraudon, Paris: 147
Robert Hunt Library: 60 (above) (National Maritime Museum), 78 (National Maritime Museum), 121 (National Maritime Museum, 146 (Musée de la Marine, Paris)
Institut de France, musée Frédéric Masson, Paris: 53
Museum of London: 111
City of Manchester Art Galleries: 34 (right)
Mansell Collection: 31, 32, 56, 82, 106 (below), 163
Musée de la Marine, Paris: 46, 85

Mary Evans Picture Library: 29, 33 (above), 43, 49 (below), 71, 132, 133, 135
From the collection of Mr and Mrs Paul Mellon: 18
Monmouth Museum (The Nelson Collection): 13, 151 (inset), 165, 170 (above), 176, 181, 184 (inset)
National Maritime Museum: front and back jacket, frontispiece, 6, 9, 10, 11, 12 (both), 14, 16 (above), 17, 19, 20, 21 (below), 24 (both), 25, 28, 30, 33 (below), 38 (inset), 40, 44, 54 (above), 58 (above), 60 (below), 64-5, 70, 72, 79, 80-1, 87, 89, 90, 94 (both), 95, 106 (below), 118 (below), 119, 123, 128, 131, 136, 137, 139 (all three), 140 (both), 142, 151, 153, 156, 158, 159 (both), 161, 162, 164, 167 (below), 169 (below), 170-1, 173, 177, 179 (above), 180, 182, 184 (left), 185, 189
Palazzo Reale, Caserta: 98 (below)
Picturepoint Picture Library: 35 (National Maritime Museum), 57, 73 (National Maritime Museum), 150, 154
The Rainbird Publishing Group Ltd: 54 (below) (British Museum), 84 (National Maritime Museum)
Courtesy of the Royal Naval Museum, Portsmouth (Photos: Derrick Witty): 39, 49 (above), 69, 93 (below), 103 (inset), 109 (above), 129, 137 (inset), 152, 186-7
Science Museum, London: 16 (below), 58 (below)
Mrs Graham Stillwell: 108 (below)
By courtesy of the Trustees of the Tate Gallery, London: 48 (detail)
Victoria and Albert Museum, London: 103, 112-13, endpapers
By permission of the Trustees, Wallace Collection, London: 50-1
West India Committee: 26, 37 (both)
Yale Center for British Art: 61, 149